Smart Dating

A Guide For Men & Women
To Dating, Romance & Sex

By
Donald Black

Editor: W. Riefling

Cover & Book Design: Darrin Harvey

Cover Photo: Sean Davis

PAPER CHASE PRESS, New Orleans LA

Smart Dating

A Guide For Men & Women To Dating, Romance & Sex

ISBN 1-879706-62-8: $14.95 Softcover
LC: 93-87561

PAPER CHASE PRESS
5721 Magazine St., Suite 152
New Orleans LA 70115

Printed in the United States of America

Contents

❧ 1 ❧

What Is Dating?

❧ 2 ❧

Where To Find Dates
& How To Get Simple Dates

❧ 3 ❧

Getting Your First Date

❧ 4 ❧

Staying Comfortable On Your First Date

~ 5 ~

After Your First Date

~ 6 ~

Being Prepared For Dating

~ 7 ~

Dancing: A Great Way To Meet Dates

Afterword
152

Sources
153

Index
155

About the Author
157

Preface

Ever wished you had a better social life? For years I yearned for a higher quality social life. I wanted to meet interesting people, have a good time, and develop lasting, meaningful relationships - to balance out my busy work life. Being around people is a natural part of life, and we all *need* to be around people. Afterall, in the end, are not our relationships with people the most meaningful part of life? You may be affluent and possess many things, but what good are they if you can't share what you have with others? It would be a superficial and empty life.

For single people, the challenge of a better social life may seem difficult. We may be more or less good at developing friendships with people of the same sex. But the world is made up of *two* genders. A quality social life includes meaningful relationships with people of *both* genders. Furthermore, everyone really ought to have at least one special someone of the opposite sex in their life. This is not old fashioned thinking, it's perfectly natural.

The challenge is how to become comfortable with the opposite sex and develop friendships. Afterall, although we are born with the desire to develop friendships with people of the opposite sex, we are not born with the capacity to achieve this. And as if this were not hard enough, there is the added challenge of how to handle the growing problem of sexually transmitted diseases, particularly the dreaded Advanced Immune Deficiency Syndrome, AIDS. What do we do?

It's odd, many people just assume that at some point they will become enlightened, or magically realize how they can approach and develop friendships with people of the opposite sex. This is a myth, and never happens. Indeed, if this were true, why are there so many lonely people?

I used to believe this myth. But after my divorce in my mid-thirties more than a decade ago, I learned this is not true. Like so many people, I had to learn the hard way. Of course, for every person who does learn to experience a better social life and develop meaningful relationships, there are many other people who never really learn such an important part of life.

As for the threat of disease, despite the efforts made to educate the public about sexually transmitted diseases, too many people still either do not know enough, or don't care enough to take precautions. Knowing how to become acquainted with the opposite sex, and how to handle the threat of disease at the same time, is a challenge all people who wish to date ought to learn.

Although I will not claim that this book has all the answers for your quest to overcome loneliness and social imbalance, I do believe you will get the basics. You will learn what to do and what not to do to get you started in getting to know people of the opposite sex in the '90s. In fact, I feel confident to claim that if you follow the approach outlined in this book, I *guarantee* you can have a more meaningful and fulfilling life.

Please read the entire book before you apply the approach I present here. There are many subtle, but important things you should learn which can only be gained if you read the entire book. You will be better prepared to succeed. This book is called *Smart Dating* because the approach is one which has been tried and tested, and truly provides the smart way to go about meeting and becoming acquainted with people of the opposite sex in today's challenging environment. Read, learn, and apply. Best of luck!

Sincerely Yours,

Donald Black

❧ 1 ❧

What Is Dating?

Dating defined by the dictionary simply means spending time with a person of the opposite sex. Dating as we know it today is quite different from what it's been in the past. About a century ago people dated only with a chaperone present. Dating was commonly known as courting. The main purpose for courting, of course, was to look for a marriage partner. Amazing as it seems, this practice exists to this day in other countries, such as in China and Africa.

Today, our Western culture views dating as far different from a means to identify and secure a spouse. However, there are still some old-world influences even in our modern Western thinking. For example, women still like being treated as special, and even appreciate receiving flowers from their dates. Perhaps some things never change. Apparently, people still have the same needs and desires no matter what the customs.

I only dated a few times before I got married at 18. And those few dates took place when girls asked me out. Oh, I had raging hormones and fantasies (just like all teenagers), but I would have prefered to give a speech in front of the entire school rather than risk being turned down by a girl. For me being turned down by a girl was worse even than death in those days.

Years later, when I was suddenly single in my mid-thirties, I may have been a little braver, but I was still not totally comfortable with these beautiful creatures called women. I still had my fantasies, and women still got my hormones racing, but I had no clue about where and how to begin to date. Could it be that perhaps I had a wrong idea of what dating was all about? Yes, I'm afraid I did.

In my mid-thirties I still held misconceptions about dating:

- You dated someone to fulfill fantasies (you know what I mean)
- You already had to love the person you dated because dating was very serious business and implied commitment.
- Dating someone eventually *had to* lead to marriage.

Don't laugh. I really, honestly felt this way. And I suspect there are many readers who hold one or all of these misconceptions.

Now, if dating is not any of the above, what is it?

Remember the definition in the dictionary: dating is spending time with a person of the opposite sex. What for? For the purpose of making a new *friend*. I emphasize the word *friend* here.

Friends

What an eye-opener it was for me some years ago when a really gorgeous blond said to me "You know how I like to be asked out?" Embarrassed, I fumbled for a response. I was so surprised by her answer. She said, "I like it best when a man treats me just like one of his guy friends and asks me to go have some pizza and beer with him. I like it when he treats me like a friend and doesn't try to impress me on our first date."

I was dumbfounded by this revelation and pondered it for weeks. This gorgeous blond put emphasis on the word *friend*. And by the way, this beautiful woman had men drooling after her - she was at least a 12 on a scale of 10. She could pick any man she wanted, and all she wanted was a friend. I finally took her advice and ended up applying the friendship approach myself. And guess what, it worked!

It took much determination to approach women as people I could come to know as friends. Before long, my new attitude resulted in all the dates I wanted. Since then, I have dated literally hundreds of very nice and quite attractive women from a variety of backgrounds, experiences and walks of life. And I'm confident that if you follow the approach to dating I outline in this book, you, too, can achieve a more rewarding social life.

No Hunk Here

Incidentally, in case you're wondering, I'm not a hunk, nor am I rich (I've been a janitor for the past 15 years), I graduated only from high-school, and haven't done very much traveling. But, unlike many men far more attractive, richer, better educated, and more successful than me, I have a terrific attitude about dating, and it shows. Women like to go out with me because we have fun becoming friends and discovering each other.

Male readers pay attention, and you will learn how to ask women out. For you female readers, continue reading and you can learn to ask men out. Women asking men out? You bet.

Relationships

The way men and women relate to each other these days is quite different from what it's been in generations past. And to learn about these differences is critical for men to learn how to relate to women and to succeed at dating.

Traditionally, women used to depend on men for their protection and support from birth to death. Now, things are different. For the most part, women are recognized by men as their equals. That is, men understand that a woman is quite capable of fending for herself. Indeed, there are more women now living life as singles than ever before. They go out and hold jobs traditionally held only by males, start successful businesses, perhaps even raise children alone.

Now, if you are a man who has yet to accept these changes, wake up. If you still believe women are only good for bedroom activities, rearing children, cooking, and darning your socks, you're going to be in big trouble with women these days. In fact, such an old-fashioned attitude will only hinder your dating opportunities. How could you possibly relate to women if you have a narrow understanding of what women are capable of?

Here is one principle with which you should become acquainted: your happiness is often in direct proportion to how balanced your relationships are with others.

What constitutes a balanced relationship? A balanced relationship is a relationship in which there is peace and harmony. And how do you achieve and sustain peace and harmony? Peace and harmony are achieved by learning about the person with whom you are having a relationship. By becoming emotionally intimate and attentive. By sharing thoughts, feelings, ideas, and so on. By learning about the other person's needs, desires, and interests.

You sustain peace and harmony by yielding to the other person, while still maintaining your own individuality. In other words, you give of yourself, and listen closely to the other person, but you don't cling and attach yourself like a parasite. You seek to please her, without groveling. You care for her, without smothering her.

Here is another principle with which you should become acquainted: your happiness can never be based on material things such as cars, clothes, houses, or anything money affords. Why can't things buy happiness? Because things diminish the importance and value of relationships with people. After all, in the end, what's most important are the people you love more than things. If you disagree with this, you're in trouble.

Here is a good maxim to remember: "We should *value* people and *use* material things." Don't ever reverse this.

> *"We should value people and use material things."*
> *Don't ever reverse this.*

Comfort

Being comfortable with someone is important to a healthy relationship. In fact, you'll find that throughout this book I point out many ways to keep your date comfortable. You will read the word *comfortable* over and over again.

I feel it is paramount that you be yourself. Likewise, it is important that your date is allowed to be herself. The fact is, your date will not want to stay around when she is not allowed to be comfortably herself. You, too, would be under great strain over time trying to be something you're not. Not only is it dishonest, but it's no fun. I'll address the important topic of comfort at greater length elsewhere in this book.

Whom Should You Be Dating?

Of course, you can date anyone you want, if she'll go out with you. But is that the way you should really be dating? Consider this: At some point in your life you have probably met someone and have had a gut feeling that something is wrong, or a "red flag" went up in your mind. Think about it, and you'll probably know what I mean.

The question is: do you ignore these gut feelings or red flags? Please don't! I'm not saying you should stop dating someone when that first red flag goes up, but I do strongly recommend that you take note of it. Here is an example of what I mean.

I had been acquainted with a very pretty lady for several years, but did not really know her well. Then one evening I was out dancing and ran into her. After talking with her for a while I discovered she was divorced. The rest of the evening we had a great time together - we really hit it off. After that evening I just knew we would start dating, but she surprised me a little when she wouldn't give me her phone number. Furthermore, I could not pick her up at her home, but we would arrange to meet for future dates. She did, however, take my phone number and explained that she didn't want her kids involved too soon. A little red flag went up in my head.

We did date a couple of more weeks before I asked for her phone number again. And again, she resisted. Up until then, I understood and appreciated her caution. In fact, withholding a phone number is a good protective measure for women to take when they are becoming familiar with a man. (In Chapter 4, I address many other good precautions women can take and men should learn to respect.) I did not complain about not getting her number, but the red flag that went up earlier began to scream at me now.

She probably imagined that I might be wondering what was going on, so she arranged for me to meet her and her kids at the house of a friend of hers for dinner and movies. All this did was make me all the more suspicious. Well, you guessed it, she had a live-in boy friend. She finally had to tell me because I dropped a few remarks to let her know that I had been here before and I didn't like the feeling. Yes, I had been there before, and so have many women I've known.

Should you seriously date someone living with someone else? I hope you feel better about yourself than to allow that. I've never heard of anyone being happy in this type of no-win situation. I have seen friends being led by lies for years, hoping for the situation to change. Finally, they get fed up and move on - a lot smarter, I might add.

Anyway, this is just one example of the type of gut feel or red flag you may have in your dating experience. You just can't assume that everyone you meet and like is the type of person you should date.

Now, why would you ignore a red flag? Possibly for several reasons. *Here are a couple:*

---

1. You are too needy yourself to be alone, so you don't want the truth.

2. The good things about the relationship seem more important than any problems that may exist.

If you use either of these excuses, you don't really have a good relationship to begin with. Expect to be treated honestly and with openness, and you'll gain respect for it.

Control freaks are another problem that could trigger a red flag. There is a saying: "The person who loves the least, controls the relationship." I believe this is true! But how sad. I personally want more from a relationship than to be controlled or to control someone else. I hope you do, too. The trick is to look for someone who feels good about herself and you'll find she will also treat you as an equal. Control won't even be an issue.

What To Look For In A Date

The first two obvious things most people look for in a date are physical attractiveness (men give this great emphasis), and a pleasant personality. So, if you're an ugly person with an obnoxious personality, you could have some trouble with dating success.

But there is something that is critical if I'm ever to get serious about someone I date. I need to see a great degree of maturity in most areas of a woman's life. I know there is no Mr. or Ms. Perfect, but the greater the maturity level, the more healthy the relationship. Certainly, a healthy relationship will have its ups and downs, but it will also feel good to be in it. If the relationship doesn't feel good to be in, it isn't healthy for you. And this will be true no matter how much you may think you "need" the person you're dating.

In the end, you will realize that only you are responsible for your own happiness. No one else can make you happy. Therefore, you have to make the choices that are healthy and good for you. If others don't agree with or understand your choices, that's okay! If they judge you, then understand that they have no right to do so. Just continue to make your own choices. Don't lose sight of this principle in a close relationship, and your experience will be more rewarding.

Dating Versus Picking Up Women

Now, let me speak to just the men for a moment. My female readers, however, may want to read this to gain insight about how we men sometimes think.

SEX-SEX-SEX-SEX!!!

Yes! That is what men-folk think sometimes. In fact, there is a saying: "Men think with their small heads more than with their big heads."

I find this saying to be somewhat accurate. This is especially true when you don't have a steady girl friend. Sex probably occupies at least 50% or more of all waking thoughts (not to mention dreams).

You women reading this are either shocked, disgusted, or just laughing at what you always suspected about men. I know at times you women can be as bad, but as a whole you are not as driven by one aspect of life. Nonetheless, it is sex that is often the all-powerful motivating force to compel men to risk so much and ask you women out.

By the way, the sex motive is also why men seem to be more concerned with the way a woman looks, than by how nice she is. For those women taking notes, what did you highlight? Did you highlight the fact that we men think so much about sex or did you also highlight the part that we first want a sexy-looking woman before we notice how nice she is? For highlighting both, give yourself 5 extra points. I'll spend more time discussing sexiness and men's attitudes about sex in the next chapter.

I wish to make it perfectly clear that I did not write this book with the intent that men just adopt the guidelines to pick up women (although the same guidelines could apply to such a purpose). In fact, I wrote this book for the purpose of encouraging people to become more comfortable with dating. Remember the definition for dating? *Dating is spending time with a person of the opposite sex for the purpose of making a friend.*

"Picking up women" is a base expression that can be defined as getting to know a woman to have sex. And quite frankly, a man who pursues women with this in mind prefers to have the sex within a couple of hours before he can get bored with the woman he is pursuing. Yes, men are that awful!! And yes, men are still doing this even though the risk to contract a sexually transmitted disease increases with every subsequent partner they have.

Incidentally, for my female readers, should you think that getting picked up might lead to a meaningful relationship by meeting "the right guy," you are dead wrong. A man who picks up a woman will never have respect for such a woman. Furthermore, such a man cannot be trusted later on.

I won't document in this book whether or not I have ever just picked up a woman (my mother will probably read this), but I will say that most single men will or might start all contact with a woman for this purpose. But a man's attitude can change quickly to a more mature one as a woman proves herself as someone worth getting to know. That is, if the woman doesn't first just jump in the sack with a guy. *Female readers, take note of this!!* Be aware that men will take advantage of you if you let them. Don't let them, no matter how nice they seem or how good-looking they are. It is not only dumb from an emotional perspective, but it is downright dangerous from a health perspective. As I mentioned a moment ago, a man who will indiscriminately go to bed with a woman at short notice, is more than likely going to infect her with a disease. The odds are stacked against a woman in this case.

What Men Want versus What Women Want From a Relationship

One big problem in the "war-of-the-sexes" is that men and women speak different languages. Anyway, there is a definite communication conflict between the two genders. I really have no illusion that this will ever be totally settled, but I know from experience that peace is possible if two mature people are *empathetic* to each other's needs and ways. Note that I used the word *empathetic* and not *sympathetic* here. Do not confuse these two words.

For our purposes here, my definition for empathy is: the projection of one's own personality into the personality of another in order to understand that person better; to share in another's emotions and feelings.

So you can make the distinction, the definition for sympathy is: an entering into or the ability to enter into another person's mental state, feelings, or emotions; this is so especially from the perspective of compassion felt for another's troubles, suffering, etc.

For my male readers, I don't know about you, but I don't want a woman to feel sorry for me just because I'm a man and can't help myself for exhibiting man-like behavior. I can almost hear the way some women think: "Oh, he can't help being a jerk, he's just a man." Although I have put up with this pseudo-sympathy a lot, I really don't enjoy it much. I grant it, you female readers who think men are so-o-o-o screwed up and insensitive are quite justified in your thinking sometimes. But have you ever considered that you may be misinterpreting a man's way? Could it be that you women are not speaking and hearing the language of us men? Here is an example:

The lady of the house spends many hours preparing a special meal for her man. Unfortunately, her man is 45 minutes late for the meal. The roast is now overdone, and the lady suddenly feels unappreciated for all her labor of love. Her man immediately realizes he's in the dog house (unless he's a total nitwit). Naturally, he attempts to explain his tardiness, but his explanation falls on deaf ears. They end up fighting, he throws the flowers he brought on the floor, peels rubber down the street, and the dogs get fatter. Men 0 - Women 0 - Dogs 1.

This may be a somewhat oversimplified example, but I'm sure you get the gist. Now let's examine this example to learn about the differences between men and women.

The man, in our example, we'll call him Frank, was 45 minutes late for several reasons. To begin with, Frank's boss kept Frank 10 minutes longer than usual to announce a promotion for him. Now, with his new promotion in mind, Frank decides to buy his lady - we'll call her Rita - a nice flower arrangement and to pick up a new light fixture at the light shop next door.

It's really quite simple: in his own manly way, Frank wanted to do something special for Rita, and he knew she liked flowers, and admired the light fixture the last time they were at the shop. In any event, time flew and by the time he got to her place he was late. Yes, Frank was late, and perhaps that was a bit insensitive, but Frank honestly meant no harm and was sincerely attempting to show his affection for Rita in his way!

And that is very often how it is. Men generally don't mean any harm.

But how did Rita respond to Frank? I dare say, much like many women probably would. All Rita heard were excuses. She would have felt more appreciated and loved if Frank had shown up on time for the meal. That's how she wanted him to express his love to her first. Then, after her expectations were met, Frank could show his love his way. Instead, Frank failed her just like men are wont to do.

Are you men grasping what's going on? You guys want to impress your women with how much you think of them, but so often it isn't necessarily the way a woman might want to be impressed. So she isn't impressed and you feel unappreciated. This is more common than you think. Men must be more empathetic to women to learn about their priorities. Likewise, women must become more empathetic to men's ways. A woman should give a man the benefit of the doubt. If given a chance, most men are not that bad.

Ultimately, we have to quit seeing things from just our own point of view to enjoy a relationship. The rewards for both men and women are worth it!

Women & Men Priority Lists

Now consider the list below which indicates the things men and women want most in a relationship in order of priority.

Top 5 Priorities of Women:

1. *Affection*
2. *Communication*
3. *Openness and honesty*
4. *Financial security*
5. *Family commitment*

Top 5 Priorities of Men:

1. *Sexual fulfillment*
2. *Recreational companionship*
3. *Attentiveness*
4. *Emotional support & domestic comfort*
5. *Admiration & respect*

I developed these lists by conducting my own informal survey. You may or may not agree with these lists, but I believe they are fairly accurate for most people.

In any event, according to my list of priorities for women, we learn that the typical woman generally wants a man who is tender, loving, and eager to spend time talking to her. Furthermore, her man should be honorable, respectable, trustworthy and reliable, and he should have a sense of responsibility about finances. Finally, the ideal man would be family oriented.

For men, the list spells out man's main interest, which we've already discussed - sex (sex was #14 on women's list of priorities). This is followed by his desire to spend time doing things and going places with his woman. A man also wants his woman to give him her attention, devotion, and admiration, and to help out around the house.

These lists reveal a great deal, and ought to be carefully considered. Isn't it interesting that they appear very different. However, in spirit they are similar. Look at the same two lists below with common connecting points indicated.

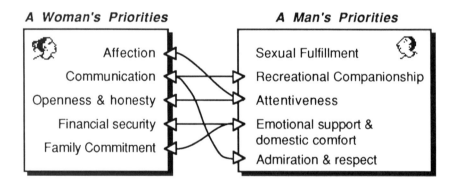

The attentiveness men want, #3, is not much different from the affection women want, #1. Likewise, the desire for a woman to be talked to by her man, #2, is not much different than a man's desire for a woman's companionship, #2. It seems that both men and women want to be treated nicely and both want a partnership when they join as a couple, particularly for marriage.

The differences between these two priorities lists is not in the content as much as it is in the application. Men and women want to be treated nicely by each other, but each gender has its own preference about how to be treated. If we use the #2 priorities of both men and women as an example, both genders want to talk to each other; it's just that men prefer talking while engaged in some activity with their women.

Now, armed with this knowledge, if you want to impress someone, and you wish to show her how much you think of her, make sure you express your love in a way that that person will understand from her perspective. Take the example of Frank and Rita. Frank would have been better off doing all he could to get to Rita's place for the meal and forget the flowers and the light fixture. From Rita's perspective, Frank's timely arrival for the meal was all she needed.

The fact is, all of us want to be loved, accepted, and validated as someone special in this world. Furthermore, all of us could benefit greatly if such love and acceptance were *unconditional*, free from judgment, no matter what we did or said. That acceptance would include accepting us just as we are, and not what we can be some day. Unfortunately, such love is a hard thing to come by.

Of course there are instances when someone wants to love you, but unwittingly you don't let her. I have personally lost a great love this way. She loved me so much from her perspective, but I failed to recognize that love from my own perspective.

We should all strive to be empathetic, and to understand the other gender so we can communicate more effectively for more rewarding relationships.

Insecurity (The Relationship Killer)

So far we've examined certain things which are conducive to building positive relationships between men and women. But if there is any one thing that I know can destroy a relationship between a man and a woman, it's insecurity exhibited by either or both parties.

I speak from experience. I've messed up several otherwise good relationships because of my insecurities. I'll bet if you have been dating for some time, you probably have messed up one or two relationships too. And even if you have not destroyed a relationship yet, you have probably inflicted some injury on your relationship because of some insecurity. However, for those rare souls who have not destroyed or injured a relationship because of insecurities - your's or your partner's -, by all means skip this stuff and go ahead to the next chapter.

For my insecure readers, let me stress that the more effectively you are able to overcome your insecurities, the more likely it is that you'll be successful at dating. Why? Because the dating experience demands that you take a chance, that you risk it all to get the dates you want. Insecurities tend to stand in the way of achieving dating success.

People who feel secure about themselves are usually more patient, trusting, gentle, understanding, forgiving, open to new ideas, socially oriented, and they have a sense of humor as well as the other qualities admired by people everywhere.

For you guys out there, women are usually drawn to a man who is obviously secure and confident with himself. Not arrogant or conceited. An arrogant or conceited man is repulsive to women. I'm talking about a man who has an air of knowing who he is and where he's going in life, and yet doesn't take himself too seriously. Someone who takes himself too seriously quickly becomes a bore.

It seems that to the extent to which a person is secure with himself, it is that extent to which he will manifest desirable character traits. Now, I've never known anyone who perfectly exemplifies security. But I have known some people who come pretty close. And they are a lot of fun, fun, fun to be around. They just don't have all sorts of hang-ups that interfere in their lives and their relationships with others.

Indeed, a person who is secure with himself is in a very strong position to deal with others. He doesn't tell other people how to think or act because he gives other people common respect and treats them decently. Likewise, he is not as likely to allow someone else to tell him how he should think or act. This makes it difficult for a control freak to manipulate or attempt to change a secure person. Someone who is secure will know what's going on, and simply ignore or resist manipulation. In short, a secure person will almost always assume responsibility for their own thoughts and actions.

Common Traits of Insecure People

You should be familiar with some of the common traits of insecure people.

Often, an insecure person tends to be either too timid or he leans to the other extreme - too aggressive, to the point of being a bully. There is no real middle ground.

Now a bully isn't necessarily a person who picks physical fights. Instead, a bully is a person who will pick on someone whom he deems emotionally weaker. The bully will nag, or be unduly critical, or he'll be just plain nasty to someone he finds timid. I have been guilty of this behavior myself in the past - a problem which cost me dearly in some relationships. But because I've recognized this in myself, I've brought this part of me under control.

You will also find that insecure people are often not gentle and kind. They talk rough and are quick to judge others. For example, they may be intolerant of an old person driving slowly in front of them and curse him, or they may become incensed when the waitress at a restaurant doesn't get the order quite right, and afterwards they treat the waitress with disdain. No one wants to be around an unfriendly, impatient, and judgmental person.

An insecure person won't forgive a wrong done him. Rather, he will seek to instill guilt in the offender, even though the offender has apologized and has shown great remorse. Nevertheless, the insecure person will forever remind the offender of the offense inflicted. Who wants to feel guilty and uncomfortable around an unforgiving person? No one.

Many insecure people are boring because they are know-it-alls. And what is odd is that despite all they claim to know, they are resistant to new ideas. It gets very tiring to be in the company of boring know-it-alls.

Another odd phenomenon about insecure people is that they can very often be categorized in two ways:

> • gregarious, social butterflies who *need* the attention and acceptance so desperately - *or,*
>
> • reclusive types who shy away from social situations.

Let's face it, the social butterfly is too shallow to be around, and the recluse is just no fun!

Being untrusting and prone to jealousy is also the mark of an insecure person. Such a person is apt to presume things that are simply not true. A man with an insecure, untrusting date, for example, may be accused of checking out another woman even if that is not true. A dispute or misunderstanding often results.

I wish to point out that jealousy is perhaps the worst of all the traits often exhibited by insecure people. The examples which follow are some of the most common incidences of jealousy one is likely to encounter in the dating scene. Take note, because sooner or later you will have to deal with such problems when you are active in the dating world.

Example 1.

The incident occurs when your date is looked at (maybe even stared at or whistled at) by others when you go out.

As long as he is not threatening, I have learned to just take it as a compliment that the looker or whistler likes my taste in dates. I feel secure and don't try to make my date feel guilty because others have noticed how nice she looks. In fact, I might even point out to my date that others agree with my taste in women. Otherwise, I let her enjoy the attention and I take it as a compliment myself.

One time some guy noticed my beautiful date and asked her to dance. I always let my dates decide for themselves if they want to dance with others or not. Well, she did decide to dance with the guy, and later when I came back from the restroom I saw her give him her phone number. I didn't get jealous or mad, but I wasn't going to be treated rudely either. So I just told her I was heading home, and was glad I had met her there because she had her own car.

What if I get attention from other women when I'm with a date? I would expect my date to be as tolerant of other women flirting with me as I am tolerant of other men flirting or giving attention to her. I won't feel the least bit guilty if she gets jealous or exhibits other signs of insecurity about such attention. I also won't take her out any more if she gets out of hand. I probably won't get mad, but I don't want to be around that sort of behavior, either.

Example 2.

Jealousy over ex-lovers. You have ex-lovers and your date has ex-lovers, so respect each other's privacy. I learned this one the hard way. The less you talk about ex-lovers, yours or hers, the better off you'll be.

Now, if you have ever split up with someone (your idea or her idea) and then later on see her with someone else, it can be very difficult to be nice and polite. Some people even start fights or make a scene. Smart or sarcastic remarks are also common during such an incident. None of this is appropriate or good for anything but embarrassment. Such behavior certainly won't win an ex-lover back, nor will it impress her. In fact, it could ruin your chances of ever getting back together with her, let alone remaining friends. It's always best to remain calm, collected, and polite. Bear in mind that the moment will pass.

Beyond these two examples I've just presented, jealousy can spring up in many forms at many different times. And this is true for all the different ways insecurities can surface. Be on your guard not to let your insecurities creep into your thinking and behavior. It it very destructive, because most immature acts are the result of our insecurities. They don't make us look mature, and they don't make us very desirable to others. This is why insecurities can be detrimental to your dating experience.

Now, I will say it is natural for most everyone to feel a little insecure sooner or later. Don't be too hard on yourself. I just want you to be aware of the effect such behavior can have and to let you know that you can control your insecurities. Here is a rule of thumb for you to consider:

> *It isn't bad to feel insecure sometimes, but it could be bad for you if you make wrong choices because of your insecurities.*

You are responsible for all your choices, as you should be. Try to remember this next time you make a choice because of some insecure feeling you have. Very often we do the wrong things because of some fear which stirs up feelings of insecurity. I've allowed fear-induced insecurities to govern my life for years. Consequently, I've pushed some of the nicest people away from me.

If you want to be successful at dating, and most importantly, at developing meaningful relationships, you must get a handle on your insecurities.

2

Where To Find Dates & How To Get Simple Dates

One of the greatest concerns you probably have, and the two things probably foremost in your mind when you picked up this book were: where do I look for dates? And: how do I get dates when I find the right people? Read on and in this chapter you'll learn all you need to know about how to find dates and how to arrange your first *get-acquainted* date, or what I call a *simple date*.

Dating Services

Almost everyone is aware that there are a variety of dating services available to help you find dates, and these services *do* work for some people. The tabloids have a lonely hearts section, local newspapers have a voice mail section for date hunters, there are computer dating services, singles clubs, single parent clubs, and the list goes on. And I feel that all these services have a place, but personally I would rather meet my dates through friends, by chance encounters, and most preferably while engaged in hobbies I like. In each of these cases I'll most likely know what a potential date looks like before we date. No unpleasant surprises.

I will point out, however, that if you apply the techniques presented in this book, you can use nearly any dating service with greater success and confidence. You'll know why I can make this claim by the time you are finished reading this book.

Places To Meet Dates

The fact is that you can find dates nearly anywhere there are people of the opposite sex. And I recommend that you are open to all the possibilities. Here are some of the best places I've found to meet dates:

- **Go back to college** and take a course you're interested in. If you meet someone there, you'll have something in common. Also, you'll know how to approach the person you're interested in. For example, ask them a question about a particular assignment.
- If you **go to church**, usually there are singles groups and activities.
- **Go for walks in the park**, and feed the ducks. Many single parents take their children there for fun and entertainment.
- **Engage in your favorite hobby**.

Of all these recommended places to meet dates, I think hobbies can be the best of the best. I've met probably 80% of my dates that way. And until you get better at meeting strangers and looking for something in common, you'll find it much easier to talk to strangers when engaged in a common, pleasurable pursuit.

But what if you don't have a hobby? I can't stress here enough the advantage of getting into a hobby, especially one that will take you out into the world possibly to share with others. For one thing, you'll be more interesting to be around. Second, you'll start meeting more people and making new friends. Finally, a hobby can actually have the beneficial effect of making you a happier and healthier person (depending on the hobby of course).

Here are some of my hobbies that have yielded many dates for me:

Books & reading:
The more well-read you are, the more informed you are, and chances are the more interesting you are to talk to. Incidentally, it is a statistical fact that women tend to buy more books and probably read more books than men. I have hardly found a woman who is not interested in what I've been reading lately. Go to a bookstore or a library and you can meet women there.

Chess:
This may seem like a boring game, but it is a fascinating game of mental skill and fun to play with women. There are chess clubs that accommodate all levels of chess-playing skills, from beginner to expert.

Golf:
Both men and women enjoy this sport nowadays.

Rock climbing:
Rock climbers call the sport "going vertical." Anyway, men and women rock climb. If you like your dates to be in great shape, I couldn't point you in a better direction.

Running or hiking:
Both sexes are into taking better care of themselves. Again, your potential dates who regularly engage in either one of these two hobbies are usually in good shape.

Tennis:
Men and women love this sport. I especially enjoy mixed doubles.

Horseback riding:
It's a whole lot of fun and a great outdoor sport both sexes love.

Dancing:
This is my personal favorite hobby, and the one at which I have had great success at meeting women.

I want to point out here that dancing is such an effective way to meet dates, I've devoted all of Chapter 7 to dancing. I encourage my female readers, and even readers of both sexes who happen to be experienced dancers, to read about dancing because there is much to learn about this singles scene.

What About Singles Bars?

Is going to a singles bar a good place to find dates? The answer to this is: that depends. If you don't already know, there are a variety of different types of singles bars. There are singles bars where people just sit around and drink or take drugs; other singles bars are places to drink and dance; at other singles bars you can engage in Karaoke (audio/video sing-a-long), and so on. The best singles bars to go to are the ones where people often go after work. These bars usually have regular, single patrons who like to socialize with the other regulars. This is a good place to meet people and *get acquainted* with people.

The advantage of the singles bar scene is that nearly everyone is single (hence the name), most likely lonely, and getting to know people is easy. In fact, even if you're shy, sooner or later, if you go there often enough, someone is going to talk to you.

One of the disadvantages of singles bars is that when you show up a few times, you are identified as "new blood." The problem with this is that there will be a number of regulars who will eagerly date you. These are just lonely people. But I recommend you don't rush things, there is no reason to get "tied up" too early. Take it slowly and check everyone out. Don't date the first people you meet. That way, over time, you can eventually go out with the best dates available. I really hope you grasp this last point. It will definitely be to your advantage if you do.

The funny thing about singles bars is that there are some really tremendous people who go there. They just stop in after work to relax and to have some friendly conversation. On the other hand, there are also the sharks who go to singles bars. These are people, usually men, who take advantage of the overly eager, lonely women who patronize the bar. For you women who are regular patrons, be aware of this fact.

Taking your time with the people you meet at singles bars is the answer to meeting people you can like, trust, and ultimately date successfully.

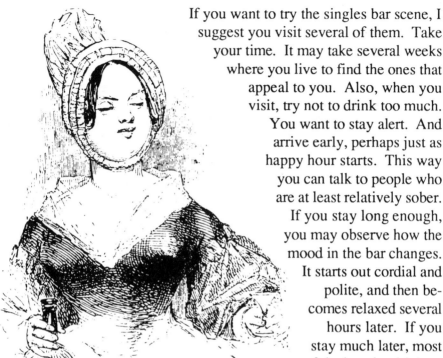

If you want to try the singles bar scene, I suggest you visit several of them. Take your time. It may take several weeks where you live to find the ones that appeal to you. Also, when you visit, try not to drink too much. You want to stay alert. And arrive early, perhaps just as happy hour starts. This way you can talk to people who are at least relatively sober. If you stay long enough, you may observe how the mood in the bar changes. It starts out cordial and polite, and then becomes relaxed several hours later. If you stay much later, most of the heavier drinkers are around, and the others have gone home. The problem with staying later is that people are probably drunk and the conversation loses all meaning. I wouldn't stay for that.

Meeting Dates Through Friends

No doubt, sooner or later you will have a friend or relative say to you: "I know somebody I want you to meet." And sometimes it's great and sometimes it's not. Anyway, I found that this is almost an untapped market. The fact is that you can probably meet many new people through your friends - possibly an endless supply if you keep asking. Here's how you go about doing this.

Don't be shy. It is really quite easy to explain privately to friends what you want from them. Just ask if they know of any single friends you might be interested in meeting. They know them from work, where they shop or go to school, relatives of theirs, etc. Then ask for the number of their friend or ask that your number be given to their friend. Personally, I prefer that they get permission to give me the phone number. At least this way I can make contact and not have to wait for a call that may never come. Whatever arrangements are made about phone numbers, when the potential date and I talk on the phone, I know what I'm going to say to get the date. (The gist of what I would say is explained below under The Simple Date.)

One of the advantages of the friend-of-a-friend route is that there is a certain amount of screening involved on both sides. You can ask specifics about the potential date (e.g., how she looks, type of work she does, her habits, interests, etc.). And be sure that you, too, will be described to the other party. All this yields the added advantage of making the possibility of meeting and dating a more comfortable arrangement. In a sense, you are not total strangers to each other. Then, when you finally meet your date, the situation is more apt to make at least the initial date successful. Trust me, I speak from experience. Let me share a couple of examples.

Just a few months ago I decided to experiment and I *changed* the procedure I've just described. I quickly learned this was a mistake. The screening process was inadequate, and I just jumped right in by asking for a full blown dinner and a movie date (which was too much too soon). (How do you know how much is too soon? - we'll get to that later.) My friend oversold me on this date and the date and I quickly discovered that we just were not right for each other. She did not appreciate my sense of humor, and we just plain did not have a good time.

In contrast to this unfortunate experience, by *following* the above procedure I met one of my favorite woman friends through an old friend that introduced us. This really fine woman worked with my friend's wife. She learned about me and I learned about her, so we had no surprises about each other. Our phone conversation went well, and we hit it off when we finally met. After that we dated five nights a week.

After about three months of this, I realized that no matter how attractive I thought she was, or fun, or intelligent, or just all around neat person she was, I had an awful problem with her son. He just wanted to throw me out of *his* house! With much regret I broke off our relationship before we got much further involved. There was, of course, no way to anticipate this.

Chance Encounters

Chance encounters can be a very good way to meet dates. Chance encounters, as the expression implies, can happen at any time, anywhere, and in any way. For this reason, you should be ready for them at all times. I have met many women as the result of chance encounters. I have dated women I met at grocery stores, at public pay phones, in the park, at the post office, at restaurants, at the beach, etc.

Admittedly, seeking to become familiar with a total stranger in a chance encounter is much more difficult than through friends or while engaged in your favorite hobby. The likelihood of getting rejected is greater. And believe me, I've had my share of rejection. But quite frankly, the risk of rejection is outweighed by the chance to date someone you find attractive. Persistence does pay, and along with the rejection, I get my share of favorable responses. Some of the nicest and most attractive women I know and date are the result of chance encounters.

More about how to approach and handle chance encounters a little later in this chapter.

Double Dating & Blind Dating

Double dates have often been the excuse for people to meet blind dates. Double dates make it a very safe and fairly comfortable environment for two people who have never met to be introduced. But

I've found that so often the jokes are pretty accurate about blind dates: you know, warts on the nose, one eye in the middle of the forehead, etc.

You should be aware, however, that double dating can be used in a way other than to meet a blind date. A women can use double dating as a means to go out with a stranger that she's interested in. The man asks for a dinner date, but the woman is shy about strangers. Instead, she can be honest and explain to the man that she would love to go out with him, but because he is a stranger, she would be more comfortable if he agreed to double date with her and one or two of her friends. Perhaps then, after a couple of double dates, they can begin to date solo. Any man who would not agree to this is probably insincere, and the woman should not give him a second thought.

Now men can use double dating as a way to keep a woman comfortable. This can be especially useful when he is interested in taking out a woman who seems a little shy. Men should always bear in mind that sometimes a woman may become particularly wary of strangers after having been hurt by a stranger before. This is something men should take into account when approaching any woman. You just don't know what she has gone through before you came along.

So, male readers, take heed! Don't hesitate to suggest to the lady you want to date to ask a couple of her friends along for the first date or two. She will instantly see your sincerity and your concern about her comfort. She will definitely be impressed by your gallantry. Of course, you may still not get the date, but rest assured, she's impressed.

Meeting Dates At Work

Meeting dates at work may or may not be a good thing to do. It mostly depends on what type of work you do, but usually it's just not a good idea.

Dating and getting involved with someone at work, may be too close for comfort in the long run. First, you will be distracted by seeing the other person at work. Second, if anything goes wrong in the relationship, this could have serious repercussions on your job, depending on the circumstances. Third, you may have to deal with jealous co-workers who may be ex-lovers or who may wish they were dating the person you're dating. They can make your life hell at work.

If you work for yourself, you get to date whomever you want outside of your immediate company, but it might not be to your advantage to do so all the time. For example, if you're a mortgage broker, dealing with local realtors, your business could decline as the result of dating realtors who choose not to do business with you once there is a break up in your romantic relationship with them.

Or if you work for yourself and you date your employees, and lose them when the relationships break up, you may find yourself constantly in need of seasoned, dependable help. This can cost you time and money as you re-train new employees over and over. These examples are not as far-fetched as you may think. I know of many instances in which these things have happened.

In my own business, I have dated customers and their employees. I have had a few problems when the relationships broke up, but to this day I have not lost a single account, even though I may have dated the business owner personally. Sometimes I expected to lose an account, but I never did. I believe my success is partly because I've always made my expectations very clear for the dating relationship.

> *Keep it strictly business.......*

In the end, my advice is that if you really like your job, or the way things run in your company, don't date anyone there. Keep it strictly business. As I reveal in this book, there are many other places to find dates.

Dating Old Friends

You may have recently entered the singles scene, perhaps because of a recent divorce, or maybe you just started to notice an old friend in a new way, maybe as someone you may want to date. Should you date this old friend? How do you go about dating her? What are the risks involved?

I think dating old friends is not a bad thing. In fact, it can turn out to be a very good thing to do. But I think you should take certain precautions. Begin by talking about your new interest with your old friend. Discuss such things as, Are we dating to just enjoy each other's companionship? or is there hope of deeper involvement? (Read about dating expectations discussed at length in Chapter 6.) The better the friend, the more you need to be very clear about your feelings or you may run the risk of misunderstanding and loss of an old friend. And don't fool yourself: there are always misunderstandings, especially when there are high expectations for the outcome of the relationship. After all, we're dealing with our often over emotional, romantic hearts.

So, talk to your friend. Don't leave things to chance. Keep in close, clear communication at all times. Then, *proceed with caution.*

I have dated and lost an old friend, so I know what can happen if things go awry. It is very sad. This is why I urge you to take it slowly with your friend if you decide to try dating each other. Otherwise, don't date your old friend. If my old friend and I had moved more slowly, we may have stopped dating before it was too late. I deeply regret the whole experience.

How To Date Someone Who Is Already Taken

Every so often you may spot someone who you would really like to date, but you learn that she is already dating someone else. It takes a certain amount of cleverness and luck to succeed at dating her under these conditions.

One way you *don't* try to date someone who is already dating someone else, is to ask her out directly. Now, you may do so without knowing she is dating someone else. That's okay. But if you're well aware that she is seeing someone else, doing this is a little underhanded. I know men have sought to date my girlfriends from time to time. But rather than get all upset about it, and go after them to beat them up, I take it as a compliment. I must have such good taste in women if other men want to go out with them.

However, if some guy just walks up to my date right in my presence to ask her out, even I would be offended at such rudeness. Would I beat him up? Probably not. But I wouldn't be very friendly about it.

Sometimes, when I'm out dancing with a date, a guy will come along and ask my date to dance. Often he hands her his business card, which she then hands to me as she declines the guy's request for a dance. There have been occasions when a date I'm with decides to dance with the guy, and I learn afterwards he very discretely slipped her his card after the dance. In both instances, I know that the women have not been impressed by the sneakiness of these men.

People will do some weird things when they are in pursuit of someone. And I think there is truth to the saying, "All is fair in love and war." But I do think you can pursue someone without being nasty, or a nuisance, or being underhanded about it.

People will do some weird things when they are in pursuit of someone.

So, how do you go about trying to date someone who is already taken?

First, if you can, ask someone who knows the person you're interested in to find out the status of the relationship she is having with the person she is currently dating. Are they dating seriously, or are they just friends? If you learn they are dating seriously, leave them alone and get on with your life. Trust me, this is the wisest thing to do.

Now, if you learn that the person you're interested in is dating just a friend, and their relationship is not serious, there are a couple things you can do.

1. *Get a friend of the same sex as the person you're interested in to go and become acquainted with her (or him). Let your friend advise you about your chances of dating the person you want to date.*

2. *Befriend a friend of the person you're interested in to learn about where and when you might run into the person you want to date.*

If neither of these suggestions works for you, for one reason or another, forget your pursuit. If you don't, chances are that anything else you do will turn you into a pest.

Of course, I should interject here that these days relationships come and go pretty quickly. So, if you're patient, and you keep tabs on the person you're interested in, eventually she may break up with the person she's been dating. This could give you an opportunity to introduce yourself. But be cautious: some people are not quick to jump into another relationship, especially when they have just bailed out of a serious one.

The Simple Date

Now that you have a general idea about *where* to find dates, let's go ahead and introduce you to *getting* dates. The basic method begins by learning how to ask for simple dates.

Simple Date Defined

A simple date is typically a brief prearranged meeting between two people who have just met (as in the case of a chance encounter) or whose only introduction has been over the phone (as in the case of a contact made possible through a friend). The meeting is usually done in a public place, perhaps at an inexpensive restaurant or coffee shop. You arrive to the simple date in your own transportation, sometime during the day time. And your simple date is limited to a cup of coffee or a Coke - no full-course meals. The duration of the simple date should be no more than 45 minutes.

Purpose of Simple Dates

To put it simply, the purpose of the simple date is just for two people to become acquainted under non-threatening, comfortable conditions. It's that simple.

Advantages of Simple Dates

The simple date is so easy to get someone to agree to, that even a stranger will do it if she is interested in you at all. In fact, if someone won't do a simple date, she will never agree to an intimate dinner date, alone and vulnerable.

Another advantage of a simple date is that once you have had the simple date, you can decide then if you are still interested in dating the person with whom you just became acquainted.

Chance Encounters & Simple Dates

Let me give you an example of a chance encounter I've had to show you how I handled meeting a total stranger and asked for a simple date.

One time I was using a public pay phone and a real nice looking woman on the phone next to me caught my eye. So, as I talked on the phone with my brother, I just checked out her ring finger to see if there was a wedding ring. Behold, no ring! I knew I had to act fast after she hung up the phone. As she started to walk away, I called to her to wait just a second. I then quickly told my brother I'd call him back in a few minutes. The following conversation ensued:

"I know you don't know me, but my name is Don." I said making this delivery with a big smile. "May I ask yours?"

"My name is Sharon," she replied, looking me up and down.

"You probably feel strange that I asked your name, but when you're total strangers, how else do you meet someone you think looks nice?" I said, smiling again. "And I *do* think you look nice. If you're single, would you be comfortable having a cup of coffee or a Coke with me so we could just talk for a few minutes?"

At this point Sharon was smiling back at me.

"Sure, I have a few minutes."

Sharon and I dated for months after that.

Here's another example of a successful chance encounter I had that led to a simple date.

One afternoon when I was walking at the park feeding the ducks, I noticed a perky young woman walking a very disciplined dog on a leash. I could tell the dog was well trained by the way it heeled. Having trained several dogs myself, I instantly recognized the dog's unusually good behavior. This made it easy to start an interesting conversation about something the woman and I both had in common. And, of course, this woman was happy that someone would notice how well behaved her dog was. After all, she had obviously invested some time and effort to achieve such a result.

Eventually, after about 10 minutes of talking about dogs and the benefits of training them, we both realized that we enjoyed each other's company. So, noticing the absence of a wedding ring, I approached this woman, Sally, for a simple date.

"I'm enjoying talking to you and I'd like to know you better. If you have time, how about joining me for a cup of coffee at Denny's right now before you have to go?" I said, smiling.

"Well, I don't want to leave the dog in the car, but I'll take him home and then meet you there." said Sally, obviously quite comfortable in my company.

"Great! I'll be waiting in the lobby in, say, 15 minutes?"

~ *LESSONS LEARNED* ~

There are several points I want you to note about how I handled myself in these examples. For the first example, the first thing I did was look for a wedding ring. To my good fortune Sharon did not have a ring, so I felt I could proceed. Then I had to get Sharon's attention and talk to her. Here was the tricky part. Since I couldn't really come up with a common topic of interest as an excuse to talk to Sharon, I did the next best thing - I talked about her. In other words, I complimented her by telling her how nice-looking I thought she was.

Now, you might argue that anyone can drool and comment on how good-looking a woman is. True, but I'm not talking about crass or crude comments. I'm talking about looking the woman straight in the eyes, and while conveying a cheerful and sincere demeanor (smiling has a way of making people feel comfortable), making a compliment a compliment and not something loathsome. Notice I used a tame compliment like *nice looking*, rather than something which can be insulting like *hot looking*, *foxy*, or something more explicit. The fact is, most women like to be complimented on how they look.

Also note that I didn't waste any time about asking Sharon to join me for a cup of coffee. I took a big chance because I literally came out of nowhere and all she had to go on to evaluate me was how I looked, how I behaved, and what I said. She, of course, took a chance by accepting my invitation to join me for coffee. I'll interject, however, that a simple date really is the easiest and safest way a woman can become acquainted with a stranger.

Now let's analyze the second example. Notice what took place and the order in which it took place. First, I looked for something that we both might have in common. This way we could both be comfortable while talking to a stranger. Second, during the course of our conversation I made a point of noticing if there was a wedding ring. Finally, I asked for the simple date, suggesting a specific place and time that would be easy for Sally to accept.

In both examples, you'll notice that I did not need to get the phone number or do much of anything else to get the simple date. The phone number is something for later, not for the simple, get-acquainted date.

Approaching Someone For A Simple Date

Like anything else in life, there is always a right way and a wrong way to do something. Here we'll delve a little further into approaching someone for a simple date.

Asking For A Simple Date - The Wrong Way

Here is an example of how *not* to ask for a simple date.

Man: "Hi! Would you go out with me sometime?"
Woman: "I don't know you, what do you have in mind?"
Man: "I don't know, how about dinner or something?"
Woman: "I guess, would you like my phone number?"
Man: "Sure. When can I call you?"
Woman: "Anytime."

Okay, the man got the phone number and that's great, but he hasn't got the date. And if he continues in this direction, he actually hinders his chances of getting more than the first date (why this is so is addressed later).

Asking For A Simple Date - The Right Way

Here is an example of how to get a simple date the *right* way.

Man (with a big smile): "Would you like to join me for a cup of coffee right now? I'd like to spend a few minutes getting to know you better."
Woman (most likely looking the man over): "I don't know you."
Man (continues to smile): "That's why I'd like to have some coffee with you and talk for a while so we can get acquainted."
Woman (perhaps now smiling): "Sure, I have a few minutes."

The difference between the wrong way and the right way to ask for a simple date is in the approach. A man or woman asking for a simple date, who is prepared beforehand, will come off more confident, mature, and convincing. Furthermore, the person being asked for the simple date is more likely to feel comfortable and inclined to respond favorably to the extended invitation.

Men Approaching Women

Here are a couple of things a man should bear in mind when approaching a woman for a simple date.

> *1. Keep the woman you're interested in comfortable at all times.*
>
> *2. Know what you're going to say ahead of time before approaching any woman you're interested in.*

These two things together make it a lot easier to get a date. Admittedly, you may not get a date every time you try, but with these and other principles you learn from this book, you will definitely improve your chances.

Women Approaching Men

For my female readers, please don't think what I've just noted is only intended for men to adopt. In fact, you, too, can approach men in the same way. This is a safe approach even though the man you may be interested in is a complete stranger. I can even give you an instance when that happened to me, and which may be encouraging and instructive to you.

Some time ago I was at a local grocery store to pick up a few things for dinner. As I walked down an aisle, I was delighted when an attractive women smiled at me. We eventually exchanged smiles again as we passed each other in different aisles. Finally, in one aisle, the attractive woman started talking to me. She said that she had noticed how I wasn't buying much food and that I must be single. I told her that she was quite right, that I *was* single. She then pointed to her almost empty basket and chuckled. The implication was that she, too, was single.

She was bold, but very friendly, which made me feel quite comfortable. Furthermore, she knew just what to say to create something common between us. This gave us occasion to talk to each other. Ultimately, she said she would love to talk to me more but had to run. She went further to say she did not want to seem overly forward but asked if I would like her phone number so maybe we could talk more later. Naturally I took her number, and we did eventually get to be friends.

This woman handled the situation perfectly as far as approaching me. After all, had she done it any other way, I might have just thought she was some sort of flake or nut I should avoid. The only mistake I think she made was being so free about giving me her phone number. To be safe, she should have asked for my phone number first, before giving me hers. I guess she trusted me, but I strongly advise against any woman giving away her phone number so easily.

It is also safer and smarter to take the phone number of a man and perhaps talk to him over the phone a few times to get to know him a little better. This gives you a chance to screen a guy.

~ WOMEN'S PHONE NUMBERS ~

My male readers should learn to respect a woman's right to use discretion in giving out her phone number. I personally know many women who have been date raped or poorly treated by men who did not know the meaning of respect for women.

A man who is mature and respects a woman will not be offended by that woman's reluctance to give him her phone number right away. In fact, a woman will respect a man more (and vice versa), and think more highly of him if it appears he is mature and respectful of her.

> *Remember men:*
> *always try to keep a woman comfortable, and your*
> *relationship with her will develop favorably.*

General Do's & Don't's When Asking For A Simple Date

Here are a number of do's and don't do's when you ask for a simple date, whether you are a man or a woman. Study these points carefully. They should become second nature to you.

~ *THINGS YOU DON'T DO* ~

Here are some things you *should not do* when asking for a simple date:

---

1. Don't get too aggressive in your attitude or talk. (A rule of thumb here is that the person you have approached may not want to be bothered. Be alert to this possibility.)

2. Don't stand too close - everyone has a comfort zone.

3. Don't speak too loudly. Loudness makes you seem aggressive.

4. Don't giggle or laugh as you speak, no matter how nervous you are. Giggling or laughing makes you seem immature. A smile is better.

5. Don't ever get discourteous.

6. Don't show too much disappointment if you are rejected. Maintain a level of maturity and courteousness at all times. After all, you never know if your next potential date may be nearby.

...you never know if your next potential date may be nearby.

~ *THINGS YOU DO* ~

Here are some things you *should do* when asking for a simple date:

---

1. Smile. Be sincere and mild mannered in your approach.

2. Keep a comfortable distance between your bodies.

3. Talk softly, but always loud enough to be heard. This takes practice, but is always important.

4. Maintain eye contact when first meeting someone. This is an important part of making sure you look and sound sincere. For some reason, men have difficulty looking other people straight in the eye. This may take some practice.

5. Be very courteous in your speech and your mannerisms. What you say and how you behave can be critical.

6. Ask for a specific time and place for a simple date. And *keep the arrangements simple!*

...keep the arrangements simple!

Overcoming Shyness

Many people reading this may think: Easy for him to do and say all this, but he's not shy like I am.

The fact is, *most* people are shy about meeting new people. So you're not alone. I used to be enormously shy. But when you think about it, shyness is just fear. The fear that others won't like you, or that you may be rejected in some way. It's natural for us to desire acceptance. Fortunately, the simple date approach I prescribe is the easiest and most effective way to get to know people. And usually, once people get to know you, they'll probably like you. This can lead to successful dating.

...most people are shy about meeting new people.

But suppose you still can't gather the courage to introduce yourself to someone and invite her for a cup of coffee or a Coke at Burger World. What do you do?

Well, I suggest that if you can't initiate the simple date approach, get someone who can to do it for you. This is not as ridiculous as it may sound. In other words, have a friend of yours set up a get-acquainted get-together. Of course, this may very well depend to a large extent on whether your friend knows the person you would like to date. On the other hand, if your friend cares enough about you and is bold enough, he may just introduce himself as a total stranger to the person you would like to date, and then set up a simple date for you. This may be stretching things a bit, but it can work if your friend has the personality to pull it off.

In my own experience, I have been instrumental in setting up get-acquainted, simple dates, by inviting a couple of women for coffee, so a friend of mine could get to know one of these women. And, believe it or not, this method does work. Nonetheless, I do advise that, if at all possible, you make the effort yourself to arrange for your own simple date with the person you want to date.

Yes, there is always risk involved when you go out into the world and try to make something work. Yes, you can go and try to ask someone for a simple date, and get turned down. Big deal. Believe it or not, there are other people out there you can ask. There are about 5 billion people in the world, and the two genders are about equally divided. Surely one of them will go out with you if you ask enough of them.

I know when I first started to implement my approach to dating that I was nervous and shy. But once I started getting favorable responses to my invitations to simple dates, I got over my shyness for the most part. Try it. It works; you've got nothing to worry about.

Breaking The Ice

Now, I have mentioned at least a couple of times the need to find some common topic of interest when approaching a stranger you are interested in dating. As I have indicated, when you meet someone while engaged in a hobby, you can at the very least talk about the hobby. This can naturally lead to approaching someone about a simple date. The most difficulty you may have is when approaching a total stranger, perhaps literally out on the street. To help you, I'll share with you several things you can say.

First, try to find something in common. I've said this before, and I repeat it again, because it just makes talking to a stranger easier. For example, the person you spot is at the same bus stop. You notice she's wearing a football t-shirt, or hat, or whatever. You could say:

"Hey, that's my favorite team!"

Then engage her in conversation about football or whatever, and eventually ask for a simple date.

In the same situation at the bus stop, you may ask the person you're interested in what the bus fare is these days. This can get her talking with you. Again, before long, ask for a simple date.

Another example may be at the park. You happen to be walking in the park and you spot the person you're interested in walking a dog. You could say:

"You know, I used to have a dog just like that."

And then engage her in conversation about dogs and pets and whatever, until you think the time is right for asking for a simple date.

Okay, these situations and examples were pretty easy. But just suppose there is just nothing in common for you to talk about. Or it just doesn't seem real obvious at just that moment. The only solution is to get real creative.

On one occasion when nothing in common presented itself, I noted how muscular this women's legs were. I said this:

"I couldn't help but notice how well toned your calves are. You must be into some type of sport; what do you do?"

I decided to use the complimentary approach to engage this person. I often do this when I'm at a loss about what to say to engage the other party. By the way, this worked, and I eventually asked the woman to join me for a cup of coffee, which she accepted.

Complimenting a woman on her hairstyle is also an effective icebreaker. Women usually take pride in the way their hair looks. You might say something like this:

"Do you style your own hair - it really looks great!"

Now, this can lead to a conversation about hair in general, and grooming, or whatever, but you have engaged this person. Then, if things seem to be going in the right direction, you can compliment the woman on her personality or her intelligence and suggest having a cup of coffee to get acquainted. Otherwise, at the very least, the woman will thank you for the compliment and each of you go on your separate ways.

Here are some other opening lines that work:

"Would you mind if I ask your name? My name is Don."

This is very direct, but it works!

Here's another clever, but effective way to approach someone:

"You're such an attractive woman, and I'd love to ask you for a date. But since I don't really know you, could we just share some conversation over a cup of coffee?"

I can hear the skeptics saying: "Who is this guy fooling? Who would go for anything like this?"

Believe it or not, many people would go for it. And if you think about it, you probably would go for it too. Why? Because it's unusual, because it's intriguing, and because it's hard to resist if you're single, lonely, and open to meeting new people.

In the end, even if it is a spur of the moment thing, always remember to think about what you're going to say before you say it, and be ready to specify a time and a place to have your simple date with the person you just met. Good luck!

Out On Your First Simple Date

Well, there you are. You've just asked that good looking woman/man to meet you at Burger World for a 32-ounce cup of sweetened/unsweetened iced tea. Much to your amazement, she/he actually agreed to meeting you. What are you going to talk about, and what are you going to do?

Should you sit there at Burger World and talk about yourself as fast as you can so this other person can get to know you more efficiently? *No! No! No!*

Is it important that you fire out 100 quick questions so that you can find out all you want about this other person? *No! No! No!*

Is it important that the other person learn all about the things you think are wrong with this world? *No!* Or worse: Should you complain about your divorce or your last relationship? Good grief, no-o-o-o! (Incidentally, should the topic of your divorce or last relationship come up, by all means, keep it as positive as possible and very brief. Nothing can be more boring.)

What To Talk About

So, what *do* you talk about during the course of your simple date? First, remember that how you conduct yourself is far more important than how much you find out about each other from the conversation. On this subject, I always think of this saying: "What you do speaks so loud, I can't hear what you say."

Here's the rule of thumb you should remember: *Always* be courteous and exhibit your best manners (but avoid haughtiness or stuffiness) during your simple date.

Also, it is very effective to have a positive attitude. A smile and good humor (and I don't mean cracking jokes) are reflections of a positive attitude. Being positive really does tend to attract people. In fact, just being positive can attract people even when few words are spoken. No one wants to be around a cynic or a pessimist. Besides, you'll also discover how your date responds to your positive attitude.

Bear in mind that one of the objects of the simple date is to learn if your date's attitude toward life is compatible with your own. Granted, you won't find out all you want to know in 45 minutes or so, but it might save you from spending an entire evening (not to mention money) later on with someone you really won't enjoy being around.

Here are some questions to ask and things to talk about:

• *What kind of work do you do? Do you enjoy it? Why? How long have you done this?*

• *What do you do when you're not working? What else?*

• *Do you have any children? What ages and sex? Whom do they live with?*

• *Have you lived in this area long? Where were you born?*

These are pretty simple and basic questions, which are easy to talk about for most people. As your date responds to these questions, be sure to ask her why she feels a certain way about any given topic. Listen to the responses, and don't be critical. Listening is more important as you get a feel for her attitude about life. By the way, later on, if you refer back to a statement she made, it shows you listened. The fact that you listened and remembered a detail about her life often impresses a person. Moreover, the mark of a good friend is one who listens.

Hitting It Off

Every so often you will really have a good time just talking with your new found friend during your simple date. That's wonderful. Of course, you may be tempted to stay more than the recommended 45 minutes. But I've found that it's much better to limit even a successful simple date to no more than an hour.

You should take leave from your simple date within the prescribed time limit for several reasons. First, you told your new friend that this meeting would be brief, a chance to get acquainted over coffee, or iced tea, or whatever. This demonstrates you are true to your word, which is important. Also, if the two of you are really enjoying yourselves, this makes the prospect of getting a big date (the dinner, movies, etc., type of date) more likely. Having a good time now implies having a good time later, even in a more intimate setting. Finally, the fact that you must excuse yourself to leave now, when the mood is upbeat and positive, makes it easier to take the next step: getting a phone number.

Getting A Phone Number

You need to learn how to excuse yourself to leave and to ask for the phone number of your new friend. Here's how you can do that easily and in a way that will make your friend comfortable about giving you her number. (Of course, there is a good chance that she may already extend her number to you even before you get this far.) Follow the examples below:

Man:

"I've really enjoyed talking to you, Sally, and I wish I didn't need to go. But I would like to see you again. Would you be comfortable giving me your number or taking mine? Whatever you're most comfortable with is okay with me."

Woman:

"Yes, I've enjoyed talking with you too. Here, let me give you my number."

Or, the woman tries to get a number from a man:

Woman:

"You know, Don, you're really a nice guy, and I've really enjoyed our conversation, but I have to get going. Look, I'd like to see you again. Why don't you give me your number and I'll give you a call."

Man:

"Thanks, I've enjoyed our conversation, too. I would very much like to see you again. Here, I'll give you my number. I look forward to your call."

Let's examine the first example to understand what has happened in both examples. You'll notice that the exit begins by the man expressing his pleasure in the company he has had with his new woman friend (in the second example it's the woman doing this). In a very direct and gentle way this lets the woman know that he likes her. If she likes him, she'll be gratified to hear this. This also makes it a little easier for the man to make his brave statement of requesting that they see each other again ("I would like to see you again"). In effect, he is setting things up for a full-fledged date.

The clincher is asking for the number. If she gives him the number, he clinches a date. If she takes *his* number, he may or may not expect a date in the future with her. I would say, however, if the conversation went as outlined above, chances are good that even a cautious woman who chooses to take his number and foregos giving him hers, will probably call him, and they'll set up a date. It is imperative that the man remains sincerely amenable to either arrangement. Should the woman only take his number, any hint of anger or frustration on the part of the man could ruin further chances of him seeing her again. So, men, I said it before, and I repeat it here: accept that a woman may choose to be intelligent and cautious about giving out her number.

What If You Don't Hit It Off?

If you experience the misfortune of not liking the date during your simple date, for whatever reason, consider yourself lucky you didn't have to spend an entire evening with that person. Beyond that, don't worry about it. You're entitled to make a mistake every now and then. Just remember to be polite at all times, even as you leave, thanking her for the chance to meet her, and that's the end of that.

A Few Words About Using A Phone Number

Men and women should consider the phone number a sacred thing. Nothing can be more annoying and obnoxious than when someone gets your phone number and then starts to harass you: lonely men who get drunk and call up woman who are not really interested in them, jealous lovers or ex-lovers who call up in the middle of the night, guys who think they're persistent in their pursuit of a woman, when in reality they are just a nuisance to a woman who has difficulty saying "Go jump in a lake!"

Men and women should consider the phone number a sacred thing.

The best way to use the phone number is sparingly. Always bear in mind that keeping the other party *comfortable* is important at all times, even when using the phone.

It just takes a little common sense and decency. For example, use the phone number only during decent hours, like between 10 AM and 7 PM, Monday through Saturday, and never on Sunday. Never call anyone in the middle of the night. And never, never, never call anyone to harass her or make a nuisance of yourself. A little more on telephone usage later.

As for the phone contact you make after your simple date, always wait at least two days before you call your new friend, unless she specifically says she wants you to call the next day. The reason you should wait two days is that if you call the next day, you may make her feel smothered with your attention. In contrast, should you wait as long as three days, your new friend may think you're not that interested. Two days is perfect. Trust me.

So, there you are, two days after your successful simple date. You reach for the phone and dial the number. But wait, what do you say? Simple. Before you make that call, be sure you have a specific date (time and place) in mind. (More on asking for your full-fledged date out, where you should take your date the first time, topics of conversation, etc., is covered in Chapters 3 and 4.)

3

Getting Your First Date

So far you have learned a great deal about approaching people who you are interested in dating. Perhaps you have even gone as far as attempting and succeeding in using the simple date approach. This is important, but it is just the beginning of becoming a success in the dating scene. You need to learn a few more things about relating to your dates. All this prepares you for the first full fledged date and succeeding dates. In the beginning, as you become better acquainted with someone, there is a right way to date the first few times. You will learn what you need to know about getting the first date in our discussion here.

The Art Of Communication

Wouldn't it be just stupendous if everyone in the world could communicate exactly what one means at all times? And wouldn't it be just stupendous if everyone would understand exactly what was communicated perfectly, every time? Of course it would. But wake up, that's not how it works in real life.

Effective communication is an art that few people really master. In fact, I've only known a handful of people I consider effective communicators.

How important is communication to dating? Effective communication is critical to successful dating. Why? Well, if you think about all that I've explained about approaching someone for a simple date, and all that's involved to get acquainted with someone, it all revolves around one basic thing: the ability to communicate. The more effective you are at communicating, the more likely it is that you will succeed at dating and in developing relationships.

Under the best of circumstances, effective communication involves using well chosen words, articulated clearly. Communication also involves facial expressions, hand gestures, and even body movement. In other words, if you know what to say, know how to deliver what you say in just the right way, people will know what you want, and will often respond favorably to you. This makes effective communication. In contrast, if you don't know what to say, fumble for the right words, don't speak very clearly, look nervous or unsure, fidget, or use some other inappropriate or awkward gestures, you fail at effective communication.

Under the best of circumstances, effective communication involves using well chosen words, articulated clearly.

Here are some simple steps you can take to ensure that you communicate more effectively.

---

1. Always know what you are going to say before you say anything. Then carefully think through the words you will use. You may even have to rehearse, like a performer, to get it right. But that's all right, because this makes it less likely you'll sound stilted and phony.

2. Use simple words to communicate. Don't try to impress anyone with your vocabulary. Just try to be as clear and explicit as you can.

3. Be careful about hand and facial gestures. Smiling is acceptable, but laughing or giggling out of nervousness is not a good idea. It detracts from what you're trying to say. Sudden or wild hand gestures can also detract from what you're trying to say. Better to keep your hands as still as possible.

4. Listen to the person you are talking to. If necessary, it can be wise to repeat back to that person what she said to show you understood her. So often we tend to hear what we want to hear.

Being Positive

Did you know each time you say something to people, you are communicating either positive or negative feelings? This is true, whether you realize it or not. Consider these responses to a common greeting:

"How are you doing?" A friend asks.

"Things could be better."

or

"I'm okay."

or

"I'm doing fine."

These are lackluster, mostly negative replies. *Try these instead:*

"How are you doing?" A friend asks.

"Wonderful!"

or

"Really great!"

or

"Fantastic!"

Okay, maybe these replies are a little much, but words you use can actually induce feelings. If you study the above replies, and read them aloud, you will actually be made to feel different by the feelings the words suggest. It's amazing.

Your aim in getting to know new people should be to convey a positive attitude. Use upbeat and positive words, and see the results. You may be surprised at all the attention you get. People will be drawn to you!

If you doubt this, try doing this for a week. Not only will you see the difference in how people respond to you, but you can actually feel better, too!

Communicating with Someone You Just Met

Let me show you how communication skills can help you in starting a relationship.

Let's assume you just asked someone for a simple date, and out of shyness she turned you down. To know that this refusal is out of shyness is something you'll just have to feel. There really is no other way to know. Of course, to someone who refuses the invitation because she *really doesn't* want to get to know you, I'd just respond by saying:

"No problem, but I *am* glad to have met you."

You may have to memorize this response for just such an occasion. *By the way, the reason for a polite response to a rejection is that:*

1. *The person you've approached will feel more comfortable in saying "no." She will appreciate this and remember it. You never know the next time you'll meet her again. And even if you don't meet her again, that's okay.*

2. Such a response actually allays the feelings of rejection you may have, just because you were polite. This may seem strange, but it's true, and really works.

But if the person you have approached refuses your invitation out of shyness, it may be necessary to communicate more clearly your intentions. I may explain to her that I want her to take her own car and meet me at a coffee shop or restaurant, just for a few minutes to relax and get to know her a little better. *I may even go further to point out:*

---

1. *I don't want her telephone number*

2. *I don't want to meet her in a private place*

3. *I don't want her in my car*

4. *I don't want her to feel uncomfortable*

5. *I really do want to get to know her better.*

Once I've communicated these things, and the response is still "no," then so be it. There will be no guessing about it. I will have made a complete detailed account of what I mean by a simple date. "No" will be "no," and "yes" will be "yes."

Most of the time all this detailed explanation is not necessary. But every so often, the person I'm interested in will misinterpret what I have said. Effective communication is the only way to clarify my meaning. As you can see then, a "no" can quickly become a "yes."

I should point out, however, that "no" can be "no" for a variety reasons, and not because the person you're interested in is not interested in you. And effective communication is the way to unearth any other reasons "no" may indicate. For example, the woman I'm interested in may truly have to go home right away, or perhaps she is with a girl friend who is driving. I won't know this unless such facts are communicated to me. Incidentally, in response to the situations I've just indicated, I might say:

"If you don't have time right now, would you like to set aside some time tomorrow or at some other time more convenient to you?"

Again, in such a case, "no" means "no," and "yes" means "yes." And again, if she says "no," remember what you say.

Four Most Common Responses When You Ask Someone Out

There are four most likely responses you will get when asking someone for a simple date or when asking someone for the first date. (These four responses can also apply when you ask for a person's phone number.) Knowing what the four most common responses are puts you in a better position to anticipate what someone is attempting to communicate to you. This is where you have your first chance at applying your communication skills - the initial contact with a person, or early on in your relationship with her. If, when asking for a date, you talk to someone in person or on the phone, *the response will be:*

◆◆◆◆◆◆◆◆◆◆◆◆◆◆◆◆◆◆◆◆◆◆◆◆◆◆◆◆◆◆◆◆◆◆◆◆

1. *"Yes," which means she is interested in you and she wants to go on a date with you.*

2. *"No," which means she is not interested in you and she does not want to go on a date with you. Although "no," as I've indicated above, could mean something else.*

3. *"Maybe," which means she is not sure. This usually means you have to convince her. This is almost like "no," and could require further explicit clarification (as discussed above) about what you have in mind, especially if you just met her and offered a simple date arrangement.*

4. *"Give me a rain check," which means "yes," but not right now, later for sure!*

◆◆◆◆◆◆◆◆◆◆◆◆◆◆◆◆◆◆◆◆◆◆◆◆◆◆◆◆◆◆◆◆◆◆◆◆

It is really quite interesting that most of the responses you will get to your invitation for a date will fall into one of these four categories of responses. Also note that three out of four of these responses are positive. And even "no" could be turned around to your advantage. So this should be encouraging to you.

What you should do is always put a response in its appropriate category of responses. This makes it easier for you to know how to deal with a response.

If you are on the receiving end of an invitation for a date, or perhaps someone just asked you to dance, be as clear as you can be, especially when you say "no." Don't say "maybe" or "give me a rain check" when you really mean "no." It makes it easier to avoid an awkward situation later. Clear communication is very important even when you are rejecting someone.

Three Steps to Dating

Briefly, let's walk through all the steps of communicating to a person you want to date - from beginning to end. Much of this will repeat what has been covered in Chapter 2, but it is good to refresh your mind before covering new information.

1. You meet someone who catches your attention.

Perhaps you spot someone you are attracted to at a party or at a dance club. Of course, as is covered extensively in Chapter 7, you ask for a dance when at a dance club. However, no matter where you meet this person, immediately look for something in common to talk about with her.

2. Ask for a simple date.

You learned all you need to know about asking for a simple date in Chapter 2; now apply it here. Listen to the response to your invitation for a simple date, and put the response in the right category.

If the response is "yes," go and enjoy the conversation while becoming acquainted with a new friend. If the response is "no," then tell her: "No problem, but I *am* glad to have met you." If the response is "maybe," then ask what it will take to get the simple date. If the response is "give me a rain check," then ask for a number, or ask when you can possibly meet again sometime.

3. *You're on the simple date.*

Just get a feel for whether or not her attitude about life is compatible with your own. Get her to talk about things she likes doing or is interested in. Remember to keep the conversation positive. After 45 minutes or so, say something like this: "I'm really enjoying this conversation a lot, but I've got to go now. Would you be comfortable in giving me your phone number so I can call and talk to you again? Or can I give you my number if that makes you feel more comfortable?" Again, listen for the response, and put it in the appropriate category. Of course, if you get a "yes," you're ready to graduate to the next step - getting you first, full-fledged date.

Asking for Your First Date

At this point, certain things have been established. You met someone you find attractive and like. Furthermore, she likes you. Now it's time to get on with your relationship with her. The first date is an important step in that direction. Armed with that person's phone number, you are ready to go into action.

To begin with, as was mentioned in Chapter 2, you want to be careful in your use of the person's phone number. This applies especially to men who tend to make pests of themselves once they've got a woman's phone number.

The rule of thumb is to call for your first date no more and no less than two days after you had your simple date with your new friend. If you phone too soon, she may not appreciate all the attention so soon. If you phone too late, she may think you're really not that interested in her. Two days is just perfect.

Before you dial that number,
you should already have these things in mind:

- *What you want to do for the first date.*
  Dinner and a movie? Share some hobby (e.g., tennis, golf, etc.)? (What you may do and where you should go for the first date is discussed at length in Chapter 4.)

- *When you wish to make the date (i.e., day and time).*

- *Willingness either to take your car or just to meet at the agreed upon place for the date.*

I suggest you keep everything simple.

For the first date, try something like Chinese food and a movie. Or possibly just getting a pizza or having burgers someplace (although not necessarily at McDonald's), and maybe drinks back at your place (although I don't necessarily recommend this for the first couple of dates). Whatever you do, don't be vague or unsure. Clearly tell your friend what you have in mind. Being unsure or vague suggests that you have not really given her or the date much thought. Besides that, it makes it harder for your friend to agree to the date when you don't know where you're going.

Dial That Number: For Men

You pick up the phone, nervous; your heart rate escalates immediately. Don't worry, everyone feels this way. Relax, because of the simple date, and the fact that you are prepared, you'll do much better than most.

Let's assume that it's a man, Don, making the call. The number is dialed. There are a couple of rings, followed by a soft female voice:

"Hello?" she says.

"Hi Pam! This is Don, remember me? We had coffee together a couple days ago at Denny's."

Notice that Don sought to remind Pam of who he was.

"Oh, yes! How are you?" Pam replies.

"Wonderful! You know, I sure enjoyed talking to you, and I called to see if you have Wednesday evening free for a date. I'd like to take you for some Chinese food and a movie you'd like to see. Would you be interested in that?"

Don is very specific here about a day, Wednesday, and a place/activity, Chinese food and a movie.

"Sure, I have Wednesday free. I'd love to go out with you," Pam confirms.

If you are a woman on the receiving end of such an invitation, and you don't have Wednesday free, but do want to date Don, make this very clear. If, however, you've changed you're mind about getting to know Don, then you have to tell Don this, or he may continue pestering you. You may say something like:

"At this time, I've decided *not to date you* for personal reasons, but thanks for calling."

For you men here, if the woman doesn't have Wednesday free, don't hesitate to ask for another day immediately to arrange a date. If you get another turn-down, and the woman does not offer you a day that she's free, then assume she has decided not to date you. If you're not sure that she's not interested in dating you, ask her. Whatever you do, if she turns you down for a date, do not pester her!

By the way, should the man be turned down indefinitely, he should be polite and thank the woman for meeting him and let it go. No need to get nasty or sound pitiful and disappointed. You never know: she may change her mind later, and give *you* a call in the future. Or she may just think you're not her type, or whatever, but she may introduce you to a friend of hers because you treated her so well.

Let's resume the phone call after Pam indicates that she wanted to go out with Don on Wednesday.

"I'm glad you do, I've been looking forward to talking with you again," Don says cheerfully.

Notice that Don is subtly romantic by indicating his interest in talking to Pam again. Don is familiar with priority 2. of the *Top 5 Priorities of Women. Women want to talk with the man they're interested in.*

"Thank you," Pam responds appreciatively. "What's a good time to get together?"

""How does 6 or 6:30 sound?" Don suggests.

If for some reason the woman does not ask about a time for the date, the man should bring it up. Just don't forget: you must set a time! Moreover, the man should have a specific time in mind before calling. It is just as important as knowing what day and where you should go for the date.

"Yes, about 6:30 sounds good to me. It'll give me time to get ready after work."

If you women cannot make the suggested time, say so, and offer an alternative. In this example, maybe 7:00 would be better if 6:30 is not good.

"Now, would you want me to come pick you up, or would you rather we meet at a restaurant we decide on?" Don asks carefully.

Don is being very concerned about Pam's comfort. Remember, they are still mostly acquaintances, and Pam may not be ready for Don to come to her home. Offering to meet her at the restaurant is a good way to make her feel comfortable with him. Women appreciate this type of consideration. (Chapter 4 offers precautions a woman can take for dating until she feels comfortable with a man.)

"Why don't we meet at the restaurant, okay?" Pam says.

"Sure, the restaurant will be great. If you like Chinese food, I suggest we go to Wong's. I can meet you there at 6:30," Don says happily.

Don is not the least bit fazed by Pam's desire to meet him at the restaurant. He's not offended that she is still learning to trust him. Also, at this time, Don suggests a specific Chinese restaurant and repeats the time Pam prefers to meet. If she does not like Chinese food, or that particular place for Chinese food, they can discuss an alternative.

"Wong's sounds great," Pam retorts gleefully. "I'll see you there on Wednesday, at 6:30. Bye."

"Bye!"

The phone clicks.

Dial that Number: For Women

We just saw how a man should make his call to ask a woman out for a first date. Now let's see how a woman should call a man for a first date. We'll continue using Don and Pam here.

The phone rings.

"Hello?" Don says.

"Hi Don! This is Pam! Remember me, we had coffee together a couple days ago at Denny's?" Pam says with enthusiasm.

Pam reminds Don who she is.

"Yes, and I'm glad you called," Don responds, equally enthusiastic.

"You are? I'm a little shy about calling you, but I was wondering if you'd be interested in dinner and a movie this Wednesday?" Pam says.

Pam pretends to be shy, just so she doesn't seem too eager or aggressive. This is not absolutely necessary, but it is a way to put a man at ease. Remember, most men are not accustomed to receiving invitations for a date from women. If a woman says she's shy, this implies she doesn't ask just *any* guy out. It makes the invitation all the more special. Of course, also note that Pam is quick to extend her date invitation specifying the day and place/activity for the date.

"Sure, that sounds like fun. When do you want to get together?" Don asks, trying hard to restrain his excitement that Pam actually has called him for a date.

"I'd like to meet you at Wong's restaurant at 6:30, if that's okay with you?"

Pam is still trying to get comfortable around Don, so she suggests they meet at the restaurant rather than have Don pick her up at her place. However, should Pam already feel comfortable with Don, she could say something like this:

"Don, why don't you come over to my place at 6:30 to pick me up?"

Like most men, Don would immediately agree to this and ask where Pam lives.

Most men love recreational companionship.

However, ladies, I actually recommend a little different approach when asking for a first or second date *if* you feel up to an adventure. Remember man's second priority on the *Top 5 Priorities of Men* list? *Most men love recreational companionship.* So after you introduce yourself, you might ask for this kind of date:

"Don, I was wondering if you could teach me tennis? Can we do it Saturday morning?"

Women, obviously it only makes sense to ask the man to share a hobby that you found out about during your simple date. But be realistic, and only pick one of the hobbies you really might like to learn. Don't do this if you are just trying to impress a man. He'll sense this sooner or later, and you may end up making the wrong impression.

As for deciding which date you wish to try, here is a general rule of thumb:

1. *A hobby date is more for building a friendship slowly*
2. *A dinner date might be a little more of the romantic type, but not necessarily (it just might be).*

However, no matter what type of date you select, or wherever you choose to go, remember to play it safe and take your own car.

For Women Who Just Can't Dial that Number

I personally enjoy receiving calls for dates from women. And I know women enjoy being asked out, too. But, if you are the type of woman who just cannot bring herself to call a man, or you just won't because you don't want to give up the control you have over men, please pay attention to some suggestions I have for you.

To indicate to a man that you want his attention and you want to date him, *here are some special ways to communicate this desire:*

1. *Make eye contact with the man of your choice, followed eventually by a winning smile. This may invite conversation that could lead to dating.*

2. *Ask your friends about the man of your interest, knowing full well that your inquiries about that man will get back to him.*

3. *Compliment the man for the way he dances (if this applies), and request that he save a dance for you. Chances are good that he will.*

4. *When you overhear the man of your interest discussing a hobby he enjoys, interject that you would like to learn that hobby some day. This is a very effective way to gain the interest of a man. Again, next to sexual fulfillment, a man loves recreational companionship shared with a woman.*

5. *Wear something sexy - this will get the attention of most red-blooded males.*

6. *Keep yourself in good shape and show it off a little. Remember man's number one priority.*

7. *Look for something in common with the man of your interest, and engage him in conversation about it. Perhaps, if things work out, and if he has the guts, he may ask you out. Otherwise, you could ask for at least the simple date to get things going. Afterwards, wait for him to call you for a first date. Many women have used this method with me.*

8. *Ask a friend to introduce you to the man of your interest, and hope he has the guts to ask you out.*

❧ 4 ❧

Staying Comfortable On Your First Date

By now you have learned what it takes to find dates and get a date. You may think: "No problem, I'll take over from here." Believe me, these steps are only the beginning. If you want to succeed at dating, you must learn how to have a successful first date, so you can have a successful second and third date. There is much to learn. In this chapter we'll discuss everything from the precautions a woman can take for safe dating to the right time and appropriate manner in which one compliments a date, bestows gifts on a date, and touches a date. Tips on getting second and third dates are also discussed.

First Date, Second Date, Third Date

Whether or not you develop a relationship will probably be determined by how well things go on the first and second dates. Generally, if you and your date got along during your simple, get-acquainted date, chances are you'll progress nicely through the first and second dates. It can be a fun and exciting time for both of you as you become more familiar with each other. However, sometimes, even after a good simple date, you may discover that your date is no longer as enthusiastic about being in your company, or worse, she's actually bored. There are ways to attempt to remedy this, such as trying a different type of dating experience, but this may not work either. If this is the case, you may as well leave her alone and get on with your life. (Chapter 5 addresses common reasons why you - man or woman - may not get asked for a second date, and what you can do to change things.)

Of course, bear in mind, sometimes it is good just to take it slowly in your dating experience with a particular person (or maybe with *everyone* you date!). These days, with the increased caution some people are taking about physical intimacy - because of sexually transmitted diseases - it is becoming common for people to date for four to six weeks before they advance from just a platonic romance to physical romance.

I recommend you take your time. Perhaps engage in the same sort of dating experience, like dinner and a movie for several dates. This is a safe way to go. It is important that the two of you are having a good time, and enjoying each other's company. Eventually, your relationship will grow and you'll get closer. This is all part of the fun and excitement of dating!

Where to Go & What to Do on Your First Date

As you've already read in the previous chapter, one good way to experience your first date is to take the time-honored approach: dinner and a movie. This is a good approach, especially if you limit it to a non-fancy, inexpensive dinner, at a not-out-too-far location. The fact is, such an arrangement will most likely keep your date comfortable. Why?

First, an inexpensive restaurant is good because it won't feel too formal, or stuffy. It won't overwhelm your date. Of course, you may be accustomed to formal dining, but most of us are probably not used to this, and simply feel more comfortable in a less imposing atmosphere. Now this does not mean you should limit your dining to fast food franchises like McDonald's or Taco Bell. The best type of restaurants are places featuring Chinese, Mexican, Italian, Thai, or Indian foods. Everyone has been to at least one of these type of restaurants and pretty well knows what to expect.

A second reason for an inexpensive restaurant is that it is not necessary to spend a whole lot of money to impress a date. Remember, the purpose of your date is to get better acquainted. A Chinese or Mexican place is great for creating a different, comfortable ambience, which is good for conversation.

A close, local restaurant is also important because female dates especially feel more comfortable being closer to home. You may think going to some out-of-the-way place is romantic or adventurous, when in reality it can actually alienate a date the first time out. This does not help in keeping a date comfortable.

What To Talk About?

As you may remember, I recommended earlier that your simple, get-acquainted date should be a time of becoming familiar with the person you just met. In a way, your conversation is secondary to your behavior. You must conduct yourself positively and be well-mannered at all times. Furthermore, you should avoid saying anything offensive: that includes abstaining from the use of profane words or crude jokes. The possible topics of conversation are simple, and ordinary. Such things as the type of work either of you does, hobbies, place of birth, children, etc. (you may wish to reread Chapter 2).

...keep your conversation positive and upbeat.

Now your conversation during your first date can go over many of the same things discussed during your simple, get-acquainted date. However, for your first date, more time can be spent discussing certain things at greater length. Again, behavior is very important, and avoiding the use of certain words is also strongly urged. Also, just as I recommended for the simple date, try to avoid talking about exes, ex-spouses or ex-lovers; its boring. Besides, if you just sit around talking badly of an ex, it just doesn't sound good, nor does it put you in a favorable light.

You may wonder *how much* detail, and how much should you disclose during the first date. Be careful here. You don't need to tell your date your whole life story in one evening. Most of all, don't waste her time with all your problems - we all have our problems. It's not necessary, and probably not a good idea anyway. Also, try to keep your conversation positive and upbeat. This doesn't mean you're limited to meaningless chatter and small talk. Just make sure you don't end up just depressing your date and leave her wondering why she ever went out with you.

Who Pays?

As a general rule, the person who extends the invitation for the date should plan on paying for the date. Otherwise, the man should pay unless the woman insists she pays, or she suggests each pay his or her own way. These days a dutch treat is very acceptable and common.

What About After Dinner?

Going to the movies is a great place to go with your date after dinner. Some people may argue that this is old-fashioned, but it really is not. Here are several good reasons why a movie after dinner is a great idea:

1. *You and your date can both enjoy the movie and then discuss it over coffee before you go home. This is another opportunity to get to know your date.*

2. *If you're the shy type, the movie does the talking for you for a couple of hours. And afterwards, the movie gives you a common topic to discuss. In effect, a movie can help you break out of your shyness.*

3. *Going to the movies is a very comfortable and exciting time that you can share together with no sexual pressures or any other social pressures.*

Suppose you don't like going out to the movies. Well, there's always miniature golf. Here are the reasons why miniature golf is a great place to go with your date after dinner:

1. *You get to laugh and talk for hours with your date. You will definitely become better acquainted while playing miniature golf.*
2. *Your date will probably relate to you in a way that she may not in other situations. There is just something about miniature golf that reveals how compatible you are with your date. You'll also quickly learn whether or not your date has a sense of humor.*

Tennis Anyone?

If you remember, in the previous chapter I briefly suggested that you could share in a hobby your date enjoys. I find that a game of non-competitive tennis is such a great way to spend a first date, that I even prefer it over dinner and a movie. I like getting out and just having fun, nothing serious at all. It's amazing how several hours go by playing tennis. Then, to make things even more interesting, I usually take my date to lunch afterwards, or maybe I have prepared a picnic lunch to enjoy in the park.

Other Hobbies & Activities

Other hobbies I've enjoyed on first dates with great success have included golf, rock climbing, hiking, and horse back riding.

Probably you'll get one of two responses from your date while engaged in some hobby for the first date. Either the two of you will really hit it off, and have a terrific time, or your date will get bored, and you'll have an awful time. Most likely, however, if your date has agreed to try a new hobby, and is sincerely interested in trying, you'll both have a good time. I just wish to point out to my male readers: always be patient and well-mannered with your female date, no matter what happens.

By the way, should your date become bored with the hobby, just make arrangements for a different dating experience next time. Perhaps just do the dinner and movie routine. That is, if your date still wants to date you.

Other first date suggestions which have worked very well for me include such activities as a visit to the zoo, a walk in the park to feed the ducks, a picnic in the park, a walk on the beach, a visit to a museum, a visit to an art gallery, attendance at a football or baseball game, riding bicycles together, and even a day rummaging at garage sales.

Ultimately, you'll have to determine what type of first date activity is suited to you and your date. You can suggest an activity, based on what your new friend has told you during your simple date, and find out if that's what she wants to do. If not, just have one or two alternatives in mind to suggest. Usually, you will agree on something without too much difficulty.

Safety Precautions For Women

A number of women I have dated have related to me how they have been abused by dates in the past. Many have been date-raped, others have been hounded by overly possessive psychos who laid claim to them after only one or two dates, and so on. There is probably more of this unfortunate type of abuse against women than most of us will ever know about. For this reason I feel it's important to offer precautions women can take to protect themselves while they become familiar with a stranger.

> *...listen closely; he will reveal a lot about himself.*

Let me interject, however, that these precautions are intended *only* for women who have become acquainted with a stranger. These suggestions are not intended for the woman who knows a man well before beginning to date him. Usually, this will be a man a woman has perhaps worked with for some time and spent hours coming to know in conversation, or maybe a friend she may have known for several years and just considered dating for the first time, or perhaps a very good friend of a friend. In such cases, the precautions I describe here will be very offensive to such a man, and do not apply.

Here are several precautions a woman can take before actually dating, but perhaps after the simple, get-acquainted date:

1. Talk on the phone with the man about different things that are important to you, and get his opinion. You may have learned all you need to know during the simple date. If not, further conversation on the phone is a good, safe way to learn more about him. As a precaution, you should not give a stranger your phone number to call you; rather, get his at the end of your simple date, and call him a couple days later. Then call him with a specific date in mind. First engage him in conversation, and listen closely; he will reveal a lot about himself. You may even decide that he's too weird to go out with. If so, don't mention the date idea.

2. Find out where the man works. If you have any doubts, look into it. However, you probably shouldn't talk to any of his co-workers or his employer, as this could just get back to him.

3. Find out if you have a friend in common with this man. If so, call your friend to find out about him.

4. If you really want to be thorough about it, and you have the money to afford it, some women will actually hire a private investigation firm to investigate the man. They can find out if he has a criminal background and other things you should know about.

Precautions for the First Date

Now, if you have taken the precautions outlined above, and everything seems okay about the man, you may still want to take certain precautions for the date. Better safe than sorry. Follow these precautions:

*1. **Don't let the man pick you up at home.** Instead, meet him at a local restaurant. When arranging the date over the phone, if the date involves a dinner first, followed by a movie, suggest a restaurant you know where other people will be when you're dropped off at your car after the date. Try to suggest a 24-hour restaurant. This is an instance when such a restaurant may not turn out to be a Chinese, Mexican, or Italian place, but a coffee* *shop. Admittedly, an all night coffee shop may not have the intimacy or ambience of the other eating establishments mentioned, but it's probably safer.*

2. *Also, when arranging the date over the phone,* **insist that the restaurant be local and close to your home.** *That way, if you need to call a cab, you'll save money (make sure you have enough cab fare!). Being closer to home will also make it more convenient should you have to walk home or call a friend to pick you up.*

3. **Consider telling a friend where you're going,** *and let your date know you have a check-in time to call to let your friend know everything is okay. Give your friend the name of your date and his phone number. If possible, you may even get his car license plate number and give that to your friend over the phone when you check in. Definitely do this if you have a gut feeling that there is something wrong. However, let the man know you gave his license number to your friend. Say your friend is very protective and insisted on the number.*

4. *When out on your date,* **don't drink very much.** *You want to be clear-minded and in control - just in case. Besides, you'll make a better impression.*

5. **Don't go to the man's home,** *for any reason, no matter what the excuse may be - even if he forgot his wallet, stay in the car and let him go alone.*

6. **Be prepared to say "no!" and mean it,** *to any suggestions or advances to which you object. And since I strongly feel everyone should be extra careful about who they become physically intimate with (to avoid becoming infected by some sexual disease), there is no reason why a woman should go to bed with a man on the first date. There are a few things she is entitled to know about the man concerning sex first. This is discussed at greater length later.*

If everything works out well during the date, relax and tell the man how positive you feel about the time you're having with him. You can then give him your number, indicating that you would be interested in dating him again. If things do not work out well, say nothing, get in your car and leave as soon as you can. Don't call him again. He probably won't call you or pester you because you did not give him your phone number. Nor does he know where you live, because he didn't pick you up. You should be out of harm's way.

I suggest women should follow these precautions (or at least the ones you think you need) with *all* strange men, no exceptions. A man who is sincere and understanding, will not be offended by this. If he is offended, he may not be the type of man you should go out with. Every woman has the right to protect herself. These days, it just makes sense. I hope you will never have the unfortunate experiences women have told me, and will meet decent men who will respect you and treat you properly.

A Quick Hug

At the conclusion of a positive, fun date with someone you have come to like even more, you can both express your feelings without being awkward or uncomfortable about it. The best way to do this is to give each other a quick hug. This may also be appropriate for the second date, too. And maybe even the third, fourth, and fifth dates. No, as I suggested above, the first date is probably not the right time to kiss or get any more intimate.

In the sixties, seventies and eighties, going to bed with someone right away was common and accepted. These days people are learning that it is not only unnecessary, but just plain dangerous. Trust me on this. Again, the timing and preparation for greater intimacy and romance is discussed a little later.

How to Get the Second Date

You have just ended a great date, and you have expressed your feelings to each other by giving each other a quick hug, as I just mentioned above. How do you get the second date?

First, if you enjoyed your date, let her know. If she feels the same, she will tell you. If she doesn't, she may say nothing or hesitate. Chances are, however, if a date did not enjoy herself, you'll probably sense this before the date is over. Remember, one of the secrets to successful dating is keeping your date comfortable at *all* times. Chances are that if you do keep your date comfortable, you are more likely to get the second date.

But what do you do if your date did not care for the date at all? Or your date does not show any interest in having another date with you? Respect her for her feelings, and just don't call her any more.

After a successful first date in which both parties have expressed that they enjoyed each other's company, the woman should say that she would like to date the man again. The couple can plan their next date right there, or either one or the other can arrange to call in a couple days to set up the second date. The conversation may be like this:

"Pam, I really enjoyed our date very much, and I hope you did."

"I did, Don. You're really a nice guy, with a great sense of humor, and I'd like to see you again," Pam says, smiling at Don.

"Thanks, I appreciate that a lot. What I'd like to do then, is play tennis with you Saturday, and I'll pack a picnic lunch for afterwards. Would you like to join me?"

"Yes, absolutely," Pam responds, almost jubilantly.

Quickly, here are the main points that should be covered when asking for a second date:

1. *Tell your new friend you enjoyed her company and had a great time on your first date with her.*

2. *Specify the type of second date you want with her, mentioning day and time.*

3. *Ask her if she would like to join you for the second date you just proposed. The word join actually makes this a non-threatening invitation.*

When arranging the second date over the phone, as a courtesy, if the man called to set the first date, the woman should call to set the second date (although this is not critical).

What to Do on the Second Date?

What should you plan for a second date? You could do the same thing you did the first time, but I suggest trying something a little different. Variety is important for two reasons:

1. *Doing something different is more fun.*
2. *Doing something different enables you to see your date in a new light. It helps you get to know her better. This helps the two of you become more comfortable together.*

So, what's variety? Simple: if the first date was dinner and a movie, try dinner and miniature golf for the second date.

What if both people enjoyed their date, but one person enjoyed their date more than the other? The one who enjoyed the date most (man or woman) should take the initiative to call for another date. This time, try something a little different for the second date. If you did the dinner and movie routine, perhaps try a hobby date for the second date. Another setting and a new experience could make enough of a difference that both parties really hit it off.

A First Date Success Story

One of my favorite first dates was with a very friendly woman I had met while out dancing. I took her to a Chinese restaurant. We really enjoyed each other's company during dinner as we talked. After dinner, we walked out to our cars. Next door was a twin cinema with two good movies playing. But I felt so comfortable with this woman, and we were having such a good time just talking, I didn't really want to spend the evening with her seeing a movie. Instead, I suggested we go to a local park for a stroll. She agreed to go with me to the park, and we took my car to get there.

At the park we walked to some railroad tracks, swung on some swings, went down a slide, but most of all talked for hours. This was a beautiful summer evening, and we put it to good use. By the time we parted at the end of this most memorable date, we both knew we had met someone special, and we became very good friends. How easy and comfortable it was!

The End of the Second Date

If your second date turns out to be as enjoyable as your first date, you're ready to go on to your third date. Again, just as in the first date, express your feelings to your date with a quick hug, and tell her you really enjoyed the date. She should reciprocate. Again, as with the conclusion of the first date, both parties should agree that they want to date again. The man should call in a couple of days to ask for a third date, particularly if the woman called to set up the second date. Remember what I said about courtesy a little while back? Each party should take a turn to set a date.

Suppose you tried a second date with someone who only somewhat liked the first date. You tried something different, a different setting and activity. But, alas, she is just as unenthusiastic a second time. If she has not already said so, just assume that the two of you are just not going to work out. This is no shame; don't blame yourself. You should just leave her alone, and don't call her any more. It's unfortunate, but these things do happen sometimes.

The Third Date

If you have advanced to the third date, things can begin to get quite interesting. In fact, you can now get a little bolder in the type of dates you suggest. Now perhaps you can go dancing all night with your new friend, have fun, and maybe even be romantic, too (although you should proceed with great caution here). But if the two of you are still a little awkward on dates together, you should probably stay with the hobby or dinner/movie type of dates a while longer. There is, after all, nothing wrong with taking things slowly. It's a fact that you can only enjoy the initial stages of romance with someone once, so take it easy and savor it.

Eventually you should become very comfortable with your new friend. Your dates together can reflect this. All-night dancing I just mentioned is one way to spend time together for a third and additional dates. But now you can also visit each other's homes. Have a barbecue, have a pizza delivered, or whatever. This is a fun way to allow your friend to learn more about you at home. Where you live reveals a whole other part of your life and personality. The two of you will invariably get to know each other even more. It's fun, it's exciting, it's romantic!

Incidentally, for you men who entertain female friends at your homes, make sure everything is tidy and clean, and to add romance, serve a dinner with candlelight. (But don't do this until you think a romantic dinner is appropriate at this point in your relationship - too much, too fast has a way of backfiring.) Also, added to the candlelight, a beautiful bouquet of flowers set on a man's table has a way of making a man seem more romantic. Women love it! (Pay attention all you guys who think being macho is what women want.)

When to Compliment Your Date

You may have been wondering when would be the right time to compliment your date. Furthermore, what would be the right thing to say?

Compliments should be approached with a certain amount of care and finesse. Like anything else, there is a right way and a wrong way to compliment. There are several things you should know about complimenting someone. First, only compliment when you feel you know someone well enough to compliment her. It's strange, but a compliment is a very personal thing, and, like dynamite, is very powerful, and you must take care not to blow up while using a compliment.

Sincerity is very important. Do not compliment someone when you are not sincere in your compliment. For example, telling a woman that you like her hat or her purse, is probably not a sincere compliment. After all, most men wouldn't even notice a woman's hat or her purse unless the hat was strange, or they wanted to steal the purse. These types of compliments *may* be flattery, and *may* get you noticed, but if you are insincere, the person on the receiving end may not appreciate your flattery. She may even consider it an insult. Boom! Your credibility is blown. (Watch that dynamite!)

Finally, don't give anyone an inappropriate or indecent compliment. This type of compliment is not a compliment, it's an insult. For a man to tell a woman: "You look good enough to have sex with," is not a compliment. It is crude and rude and reduces the woman to nothing more than an object. The only time this might be an exception is if the man and woman are already very intimate and know each other very well. Nonetheless, better safe than sorry. Better off not detonating another stick of dynamite!

Compliments must be sincere and non-insulting. What does that mean? A sincere, respectful compliment is not intended to simply draw attention to yourself, or to try to win favor, but is a positive expression of your thoughts out loud.

A respectful compliment should not be limited to comments on how someone looks. This often only amounts to flattery. Generally, compliments should be focused more on the positive character attributes of a person. For example, if appropriate, you may tell someone: "You are a very disciplined person, and I admire that in you" or "I really appreciate your attitude and sense of humor in this situation." These compliments are more specific and more meaningful to most people.

Don't misunderstand: there is nothing wrong with telling someone you've known for some time that she looks pretty, or whatever; just use this type of compliment sparingly. Then, perhaps after you've persuaded her that you are truly impressed with her character, she might be all the more appreciative of any compliments you make about her physical appearance.

I will interject here a couple of acceptable conditions when you may employ flattery, albeit with discretion. For one thing, flattery of a person's physical appearance may be all you can come up with as you grope for some words to say when you have just spotted someone you'd like to know. But you can get much further if you can say something positive about her character. Also, flattery of a person's physical appearance may be useful when you're out at a dance club and wish to gain the attention of someone you're interested in. At a dance club I've learned that this works and is acceptable. Of course, not everyone you compliment or flirt with will necessarily respond favorably toward you.

When to Bring Flowers and Other Gifts

Most everyone enjoys receiving gifts and flowers (yes, even men can appreciate flowers). In the dating environment, as we just learned with compliments, you have to be careful not to overdo it. In other words, what you give depends on how far along you are in your relationship with someone. If you are too extravagant early on, you create the impression that you are trying to show off how much money you have, or that you're too eager to impress, to make things move along too quickly. This can actually impede progress.

At the beginning, keep it simple. A small gift of flowers is not unacceptable. Later on, once you become more familiar with your date, and you want to be a little romantic, you can bring flowers and a card. The card might read: "To a new friend whom I've grown fond of." Hallmark Cards has a variety of "friendship" or "new-love" cards on the market. Women have done this for me, and I've always felt quite comfortable about receiving such a thoughtful gift.

If you've just been catapulted into a full-blown love affair, by all means express your love by getting something extremely extravagant at least once. This will help the commitment be more fun and exciting. Some suggestions? If it's Valentine's Day, bake a giant chocolate cake in the shape of a heart. Or you could also buy jewelry, like a nice necklace or bracelet, for a woman who likes those things.

When to Touch Your Date

By the word touch, I don't mean sex. I mean holding hands, or kissing, or hugging. Of course, once the touching begins there is no telling where it may end (but try to control yourself at least for your own physical health). What I wish to address here, mainly, is the approach to touching your date, and how both parties can remain comfortable through the whole experience.

Touching usually begins in two ways: touching either comes easily, or it doesn't come easily. But try to keep this thought in mind:

"It is better to be a yard behind, than an inch too far."

So it is with touching for the first time. It can be better to wait too long than to touch too soon and make your date uncomfortable.

It is always nice to give a friendly hug goodbye at the end of a date. This is even acceptable at the conclusion of the first date. Either party, the man or the woman, can be the initiator of such a hug.

But when it comes to the first kiss, be careful. I recommend that the man let the woman lead on this. The woman should indicate to a man that she would like to be kissed. She can either suggest that he kiss her, or she can avail herself by leaning closer to the man when he's talking. Another way a woman can indicate to a man that she is receptive to letting him kiss her is to kiss him on the cheek when saying goodbye at the end of a date. The man can then attempt to kiss the woman, or he can wait until the next date to give it a shot. Another effective way for a man to find out if a woman is receptive to him for a kiss, is for him to simply ask her. Men, memorize this:

"Can I kiss you?"

Pretty simple. But I have personally learned that this is often one of the best ways to keep my date comfortable when trying to kiss her. Consider this: I'd rather be told "no" than be rejected and pushed away.

What about holding hands? Holding hands can either be boring or a very exciting experience if you're with the right person. But again, as with kissing, be careful. You don't want to try this too soon. I suggest holding hands be reserved for after you have successfully kissed your date. Of course, this does not mean you can't or should not hold hands before kissing. I just believe holding hands is a natural expression of the romantic feelings that result from kissing. It's logical to me that one should follow the other. It's also more fun and exciting.

"Can I kiss you?"

❧ *5* ❧

After Your First Date

Although in Chapter 4 we spent time discussing first, second and third dates, we have not thoroughly discussed why sometimes you can't get a second date or maybe the third date, even when things seem to be going all right. Furthermore, we'll explore in this chapter how to handle such things as getting serious about someone you're dating, sleeping with someone, and managing a breakup - should it occur - and remaining friends.

Why Men Don't Ask a Woman out for a Second Date

There may be any number of reasons a man may not ask a woman out for a second date. We'll bring up here some of the most common reasons and what if anything you can do to change things.

Unfortunately, one of the most common reasons a man won't ask a woman out for a second date has nothing to do with the woman. As tragic as it is, many men go out with a woman only for the purpose of having sex with her. And it often happens that when such an insincere man dates a woman, and she does not submit to his desire, he immediately loses interest in her. He'll just go on to the next woman. Eventually, he'll get what he wants. Yet, this type of man is often still not satisfied, and he just goes on to the next woman who is willing to sate his desires. And he goes on to the next, and to the next, and to the next. That's why many men just don't get married. Why should they? If women sooner or later give them what they want, they go living single lives just as they please.

So, ladies, don't fret too much if a man does not call you again. Chances are he just didn't get what he wanted, and couldn't be bothered with you. Therefore, you should not bother with him.

Now, of course, there may be another, perhaps more complex reason a man may not ask you out again. For example, the man's old girlfriend found out that he went out with you. Suddenly, he regains her interest, and you become history. Or perhaps the man finds out you're Catholic, and he hates Catholics. He drops you without a second thought. When it's a complex reason, there's nothing you can do about it. So, just go on with your life.

However, there are a number of simpler reasons a man may not ask a woman out again. Study the list here, and evaluate yourself to determine if you're guilty of any of these offenses. If you are, these are things you can do something about:

◆◆◆◆◆◆◆◆◆◆◆◆◆◆◆◆◆◆◆◆◆◆◆◆◆◆◆◆◆◆◆◆◆◆

- Did you get too flirtatious with other men while out on your date? You have to decide whether or not you're interested in the man you're with. That shouldn't be too hard to decide.

- What kind of language did you use? If it was profane, that may have been offensive to a man, even if he used profane words himself (it's odd, but men *do* have double standards).

- What kind of mood were you in? Were you edgy, mean, irritable? Yes, *all* people are fully capable of controlling their behavior if they really want to.

- Were you full of energy, or were you dragging? Going out in the evening after a full day at work can be tiring.

- How was your breath? Believe it or not, some people get very turned off by people with bad breath. Nothing a breath mint or spray can't handle.

- Did you talk negatively about your ex-lover or ex-husband? Exes are not a good topic, no matter how you put it.

- Did you talk negatively about other people? Talking negatively about other people makes you out to be a gossip. This is not appealing to some people.

- Did you monopolize the conversation all evening? Don't just chatter away. Try to respond to questions, and don't just talk without giving your date a chance to talk.

- Did you insist on your own way? For example, did you insist that the two of you see a particular movie, no matter what? Being pushy is not attractive - in women, it makes them seem bitchy.

- Were you well-mannered while eating? Who wants to eat with a slob? - food particles flying, lips smacking, greasy fingers, ad nauseam.

- Were you dressed appropriately? Underdressed, overdressed? Men are usually worse at this than women, but sometimes it is surprising how women will dress.

- Did you conceal your boredom? Look, no matter how good-looking he is, if the guy is a bore, he's probably not for you. Who wants to be around a bore?

- Did you remain overly private, refusing to talk about yourself very much? This is the other extreme to spilling your guts about everything in your life from day zero. Neither extreme is good.

- If your date was 10 or 15 minutes late, did you make a big deal about it, trying to make him feel guilty? Who wants to be nagged at on just the first date?

- Did you smoke? Unless you've been living in a cave the last couple of years, fewer people are tolerant of smokers. Try to abstain from smoking, or at least ask permission from your date, or wait to smoke outside, alone. Better yet, quit; it's a nasty, expensive habit anyway.

- Did you reveal to your date that you enjoy using certain recreational drugs? If so, that could be enough reason for a man to lose interest. More and more people are coming to the realization that drug use is stupid.

◆◆◆

Naturally, this list could go on and on. But for the most part, I believe these represent some of the most common, simpler problems that reduce the chances of getting a second date with a man.

But what if you're not sure about why a man won't ask you out for a second date? Well, one way to find out is to call him and ask. If it's because he just wanted sex or it's some goofy complex reason, he may not give you a straight answer. On the other hand, he may be honest and tell you he was offended that you smoke, or that you played with your food, or whatever.

Obviously, if you discover that you do something that turns people off, you can learn to stop doing it.

I can think of a number of past dates who had a variety of problems. And it's not that I'm just picky, either. Let me tell you about a few of them.

I've dated women who couldn't stand their children. But what did they talk about? Their kids! All evening long it was, My kids this, or My kids that. On and on. I never called them again.

I've dated a few women who overdressed for just going to a Mexican restaurant and a movie. And all the while they were unbelievably haughty and full of themselves. What bores! I never called them for a date again.

I've dated some women who I suppose were so nervous about dating that they couldn't stop talking, and talking, and talking...

I've dated women who could talk about nothing else but their ex-husbands. He didn't pay child support, he was so cheap, he was a cheat, he was lazy, he used drugs, he wasn't a good father to his children, he - and on and on it went.

I know I have a pretty good sense of humor. And I easily get along with people who are happy, or at least have a sense of humor and just don't take life so damn seriously. Well, one date I had just didn't know what having a sense of humor was. She just didn't get my humor at all. I kept thinking, "Good grief, lighten up already!" But she wouldn't. In fact, it even went so far that she became irritated with me a couple of times. I decided not to call her again.

Now, here's the interesting thing about recognizing that you behaved inappropriately, or that you spent too much time chattering about the wrong thing, or whatever: you *can* make an effort to patch things up. And it *can* work. One case in point is this last woman who apparently had no sense of humor. Well, it turns out, after two weeks of not hearing from me, she must have realized that I wasn't going to call her. So she called me and invited me to a barbecue. Why I went, I'm not sure. Anyway, amazingly enough, I had a great time, and discovered that she was not so bad. In fact, we dated for months after that. She was a great person. We just got off to a rough start. Of course, had she never taken the initiative to restart our friendship, we probably would have never seen each other again.

You may wonder if this woman developed a sense of humor overnight. Let's put it this way: she may not have been able to generate humor, but she could at least appreciate it as she came to appreciate the sort of person I was.

Why Women Won't Go out with a Man on a Second Date

Okay guys, you call the woman again and again, but she's not there, or she doesn't return your call. What went wrong? Here is a list of common problems men are often guilty of; problems that can thwart the chances of a second date with a woman. Men, study this list, and evaluate yourself to determine if you perpetrated any of this type of behavior:

- Did you drink too much? Amazing as it may seem, some men actually think it is attractive and macho to show women that they can hold their liquor, even when imbibing in vast quantities. Women couldn't care less how much you can drink.

- Did you brag about yourself, on and on? You did this, and you did that, etc. How boring.

- Were you *overly* sweet with your compliments? It doesn't take long for a woman to become suspicious of your sincerity if you keep this up.

- Did you flirt with other women? Men, if you're out with a woman, the least you could do is give her your full and undivided attention. Flirting, and even letting your eyes wander as you check out other women, is very offensive to most women.

- Did you dress appropriately? I believe men are getting better in this area, but it still amazes me when a woman dresses attractively, and a man just throws on some partially clean T-shirt and jeans. Women *do* notice what a man wears.

- Did you get too serious for a first date? Professing your unwavering devotion to the woman, declaring you want her to bear your children, or some other nonsense, can make you look like a fool. Besides that, you can seem immature, desperate, and perhaps even insincere.

- Did you try to make an impression with your money? Some men want to impress women with all their money. These men may flash several one-hundred-dollar bills in their wallets, leave gargantuan tips, boast openly about how much money they make, or perhaps insist on paying for everything even when a woman indicates she would like to pay her way. Although a woman may like the idea that a man has some means, when it is obviously shown to impress, it can be a big turn-off. I suggest you big shots and millionaires remain conservative. Your money and achievements are far more impressive when a woman discovers them gradually, and you don't make a big deal about them.

- Did you complain about having to pay child support? In other words, did you start griping about your ex-wife and your kids? If so, you're a bore. Best to keep ex-anyone out of your conversation.

- Did you bathe before going out? This goes along with appropriate dress. It amazes me when men just assume they are clean enough. They don't realize how sensitive most women are to men who are not clean. If you have not bathed for a while, you can look bedraggled and give off an unappetizing odor. Trying to disguise yourself with cologne or deodorant may work once in a while, but women will eventually get wise to such a habit.

- Were you a gentleman who opened doors? No matter what you hear about feminism, women love to be treated special. They are born romantics. Opening doors is easy, but considered by women an important romantic gesture. Men, do it; it's not that difficult.

- Did you get too "friendly" during the first date? What I mean here is, did you make a pass, or assume you were entitled to a kiss, or more? Reread Chapter 4 to learn about touching your date. The first date is not the time for such friendliness. Besides, it's not your decision to make; it's up to the woman.

- Did you *listen* to the feelings your date shared? Women are feelings-oriented, and men should learn to be sensitive to this. Listening not only means keeping your ears open, but it also means being attentive and focused on your date, without passing judgment. This can mean a great deal to a woman.

- Did you boast of macho exploits and fighting adventures? This is a weird one, but something many men are into. Many men fantasize about being James Bond, or some other action hero. They imagine that they can take on a dozen other men in hand-to-hand combat at bars, or that they are not afraid to stare down a big brute at a ball game, or whatever. Somehow, like holding their liquor, or showing off muscles or how much money they can spend, men often think women are impressed by machismo and fighting. Wrong! Most women are repulsed by this, and would rather listen to some poetry you wrote, or hear your opinion about a meaningful novel you have read.

◆◆◆◆◆◆◆◆◆◆◆◆◆◆◆◆◆◆◆◆◆◆◆◆◆◆◆◆◆◆◆◆◆◆◆◆◆◆

Of course, smoking and using drugs are another couple of things men should avoid doing or discussing on a first date. Being well-mannered while dining is also a good idea. Anyway, as with the list for women, this list can go on. Although I think generally this list covers some of the more common offenses exhibited by men on a first date. If you are guilty of any, or several, or all of these, try to change your evil ways. You'll benefit if you do.

Ultimately, the lesson you can learn is that if you insist on being rude or impatient, exhibit unacceptable habits, remain selfish or negative or pushy, or demonstrate some other unappealing behavior, you cannot expect to get past the first date. In fact, it's amazing if you even get that far. However, should you realize where you went wrong and decide to change, I guarantee your dating experience will dramatically improve. You'll get past the first date without too much difficulty.

Now, you may think being on your best behavior will wear you out. It could be a strain, but everyone has shortcomings. The trouble is when we allow too many shortcomings to come out too early in a relationship. It is not dishonest or insincere to be on your best behavior while becoming familiar with someone. It's just practical, common sense. Eventually, the less savory side of your disposition will surface. But at least in the meantime, I hope you will have had enough time to demonstrate to the other party that you're not so bad. You may have flaws, but none that others can't live with. After all, they will have to realize that they, too, have flaws. It's all part of being human.

Getting Serious about a Date

Suppose things are rolling along just nicely between you and your new friend. First date, second date, third date, and all is fine. Now what? Well, the direction your relationship goes depends entirely on how you and your friend want it to go. You'll have to ask yourselves what you want out of the relationship. What are your expectations? (Various expectations and their implications are discussed at length in Chapter 6.)

The moment two people start having sex together,
everything is different.

Apart from the diseases to which one is susceptible when having sex with someone, sex has a way of completely changing the way people relate to each other. The moment two people start having sex together, everything is different. This can be one of the most wonderful experiences in a relationship, or it can be the most disastrous. Often the unsavory sides of personalities begin to surface. Pet peeves, jealousies, and all sorts of weird things come out.

Also, in my observance of relationships as they develop, particularly after sex has entered the picture, there is often the tendency of one party to become more serious, attached, or infatuated than the other. In other words, an imbalance often occurs in the relationship - it just becomes too one-sided.

You can identify signs of one-sidedness in a relationship when one person:

- *gives more* love and affection than the other
- *apologizes more* often than the other
- *struggles more* than the other to make the relationship work and remain positive
- *sacrifices more* than the other (vis-a-vis feelings, money, friends, family, fun, etc.).

If your relationship seems to be going in this direction, perhaps getting serious is not a good idea. Why? Chances are that you'll never overcome this imbalance. This is sad. Of course, you'll have to decide for yourself what to do in such a relationship.

However, if after sizing up your relationship you decide to get serious, you probably want to have sex with your new friend. We live in dangerous times, and there are some things you should discuss with your friend, and ways to prepare for sex so you can protect yourself. In Chapter 6, study the discussion on how to approach sex the *smart* way.

Now, if your relationship is going in a positive direction after sex has entered the picture, and you still like each other, by all means, don't stop dating the way you were before. In fact, make a special effort to go on hobby dates. These dates still help bring you and your friend closer as you share in a common interest (no, sex does not qualify as a hobby). You'll find that a good friendship is reflected in better romance.

...make a special effort to go on hobby dates.

How to Break Up and Still Remain Friends

Is it possible to get serious with someone you've been dating, then end the relationship and still remain friends? There are two ways to address this concern.

---

1. If you have not had sex, and no longer wish to date the person you've just started to know, you can still be friends. At the very least, you can be civil and polite to each other, and maybe even date at some time in the future.

2. If sex has already entered the picture, remaining friends is very difficult if the two of you decide to part ways.

As I said earlier, sex changes everything between a man and a woman. The two parties either treated each other well before and after sex entered the picture, or they treated each other poorly. As a rule, should a man and a woman who treated each other well before and after having sex decide to part ways, they are more likely to remain friends than a couple who treated each other poorly. But even under the best of circumstances, neither party may want to be friends after a breakup.

Some common reasons that people break up and stay apart without ever reconciling include the following:

- *One person began dating someone else before the break up*
- *One person overly dominated and manipulated the other person*
- *Either one or both parties exhibited too many emotional problems in the relationship, particularly in the form of anger or jealousy*
- *Alcohol or drug abuse interfered with the relationship*
- *Either one or both parties were consummate liars or possibly even thieves.*

The list could go on, but these are probably the more common reasons for a breakup, and they are the ones that would make it very unlikely that a man and a woman would remain friends.

In my own experience, I have ended relationships and can attest to both women who sustained polite friendships with me and others who would have nothing to do with me any more. In contrast, there are cases in my own life when women ended the relationship and I wanted nothing to do with them, while other women still have lunch with me from time to time. Each situation is different, and you'll just have to decide for yourself what to do in a particular case.

Can You Win Back Someone You Once Dated?

I've heard it said that you should never go back, because it never works. And so far, most of the time, I have found this is true. Why? The reason that broke up the relationship to begin with is very likely the same reason it won't work a second time, either. This argument applies to third and fourth tries, too. Unless the problem is dealt with, I have found it is a waste of my time and emotional energy to try again.

Very often the problem is not the fault of just one person. Usually, the fault exists with both parties in one way or another. For example, one person seeks to dominate the other for her/his attention, while the other is too selfish to yield. Both are at fault. One has to dominate less, and the other has to give more. If this is not cleared up, the relationship won't last, and trying again without any change in behavior on the part of both people won't help either.

Of course, in order to try again, both people must understand the problem. Then both have to seek to change themselves. This is an active, participatory process for both people. It cannot be done by just one person. It is unhealthy to have an imbalanced, one-sided relationship. Unfortunately, it can be very difficult, often impossible, for two people to come to such an agreement and make it work.

Then, there is the problem of trying to persuade the other party even to consider the idea of coming back and trying again as I've just suggested. How do you communicate with someone who is more or less bent on forgetting the relationship?

You could try a dozen roses sent to the solicited party. Both men *and* women can try this. This has actually worked on me when a woman I broke up with sent me one dozen, and then a second dozen roses to get my attention. The second dozen did the trick. And, yes, I agreed to meet with the woman and listen to her.

Another way you may regain the attention of the other party is to convey a heartfelt apology. This can work only if you were fairly well behaved on the way out of the relationship. You have a chance if you were mature and did not pick the other person apart, or unload all your petty gripes, or make a nuisance of yourself with repeated phone calls or visits to the other person's workplace, or incessantly whimpered, whined and groveled, or displayed other reprehensible conduct. Bear in mind, however, that if you hurt someone deeply enough, it may not matter how heartfelt the apology. Immature behavior can actually make it easier for the other person to leave and never look back.

What about using sex to win someone back? Some women do this. They want a man who has dumped them, and they know what a man likes: sex. So, to lure the man, they let the man take his pleasure with them. This is not a good idea. A man may take advantage of the opportunity for sex, but he can still be detached and unconcerned about the relationship. I know people whose relationship is based only on the sex they have. This is not the basis for a healthy, happy, sustained relationship. There is much more to life shared with another person than just sex.

6

Being Prepared
For Dating

There are a number of miscellaneous topics that are important for you to consider to be better prepared for successful dating. These topics range from what your expectations are of dating, to sexual relations, to personal grooming, to your feelings about kids, and even to the car you drive. These and a number of other topics that I think are important concerning dating are discussed in this chapter.

Great Expectations

Everyone who dates has some type of expectations of what dating will provide. Many men are just out to find someone to sleep with. This is unfortunate, but a reality women have to accept. However, many other people - male *and* female - are looking for a companion, a friend, or perhaps even a mate. The question you should ask yourself, before you go out to meet people for dating, is: "What do I expect from my dating experience?" Knowing what you want will help you as you relate to the person or persons you date.

As a rule of thumb, you should not expect any more from someone you're dating than what the two of you have already discussed and agreed to. This may sound very clinical and unromantic, but it is a smart way to conduct a relationship. Why? It makes things clear to both parties about the direction of the relationship. Let me give you a simple example.

Suppose at the outset of your relationship with your new friend, you agree to go out to dinner together. Fine. And suppose that's all you agree to. If that's all you expect, no problem. However, if suddenly you expect that your date be committed to only you from the time of the dinner date on, you have overstepped the bounds of what you agreed to with her. You'll probably end up disappointed or angry when you learn that your date is dating someone else.

People are funny. They complain to the other person, saying, "I expected you to know how I felt about that!" Oh, really? If people could read each other's minds, maybe so. But that's not how it works. You must voice your expectations so the other person knows how you feel and what you want. Remember how I emphasized the need for clear and direct communication earlier in this book? This is where communication applies again. In fact, the need for clear communication never really ends.

The advantage of discussing and agreeing to what to expect in the relationship is that you lessen the chance of disappointment and problems in the relationship. To really keep things simple, I suggest you *just don't expect <u>anything</u>*! Or at least don't expect very much.

Now you may think: But this sounds so cynical, so unfeeling! True. But trust me, it's one of the safest ways to protect yourself from hurt.

If you take this recommended approach, you will progress gradually from one stage of the relationship to another without much misunderstanding, embarrassment, frustration, and other emotions that often hinder the development of most relationships. I know this to be true because of my own bumbling efforts at relationships. I painfully recall when I jumped to page 10 in the book-of-love, while the woman I had been dating was still back at page 5. What an embarrassment it was to me when she did not respond in the way I expected her to. Why? Because I did not clearly communicate my expectations, and we did not agree about where we were in our relationship.

Give the person you're dating some time and freedom to enjoy your relationship. Allow your relationship to develop gradually. Why rush it?

A budding romance only happens once. Take your romance, and all the other wonderful things a relationship can be, slowly. Savor it like a good, expensive glass of wine.

Neediness

In general terms, there are two reasons a person may be in a relationship:

1. *because of neediness, as in the case of a person who seeks out another person to meet a certain unfulfilled need within himself/herself (e.g., a desire to feel secure after a lifetime of feeling insecure and unloved)*

2. *because of a genuine admiration of and interest in another person on the basis of who that person is, which makes one seek to cultivate a lasting relationship with him or her.*

It is the latter of these two reasons that is the healthiest and most likely to endure. The problem for the needy person is that not only does his neediness create a strain on a relationship from the beginning, but should the needy person mature over time, he can outgrow the relationship. In other words, he could reach a point where he no longer needs the person with whom he has been relating.

It is a myth to assume that one can meet the "right person" who will "make" him happy. True, he may find someone suited to him, and from that standpoint, that is the right person. But to expect someone else to "make" one happy is a mistake. The fact is, no one can make another happy. One has to find happiness or contentment within himself. This may be a lifelong pursuit, and I think it involves much more than just relationships with others, or the attainment of certain material achievements. It is physical, emotional, and spiritual.

Ideally, each person should seek to enter into a relationship in which there is a mutual attraction and interest in the other party, not for what that person can do, but for who that person is. This way, should the parties involved each mature (which is a normal part of experiencing life), they are likely to continue an enjoyable mutual interest and appreciation for each other. This can result in a healthy, lasting relationship.

If a person is basically happy or content, he will attract people. I have been such a person, and the exact opposite. In the past I have been a drain on others around me, because I sought happiness and fulfillment through my relationships. Now, I consider myself a happy person, not really expecting anything of anyone. I have found that people are more drawn to me. Has this helped my outlook on life? You bet. Has this helped out my dating experience? Absolutely!

But suppose you find yourself in a relationship with a person who is obviously needy. Is there anything you can do about it? The best way to address neediness is to confront it openly. Discuss the needs. Point out the difficulty that meeting those needs can create for you. Ultimately, discuss ways you can work out a solution to his or her needs without perpetuating a strain on your relationship. Just ignoring or hiding neediness is not going to address the problem or make it go away.

Exclusivity

We touched on the tendency for people to expect an exclusive dating arrangement. This can be something of great concern to a couple. Again, if you expect that your friend will date only you, let her know this. If you are open-minded, this won't be an issue in the first place.

Perhaps you want to date others while dating someone. Should you expect exclusivity from the person you're dating? I don't think so. Be fair and reasonable. Be open and honest.

Keep in mind that exclusivity means commitment. Not everyone is ready for commitment, for whatever reason. You cannot *make* someone commit. If you want to have an exclusive relationship with your friend, and she doesn't, you should either accept this or simply stop dating her.

But what if you're sleeping together? Doesn't this naturally establish exclusivity? Not necessarily. Just because you sleep with someone does not mean you can now expect her to do or not do certain things. Sex and its effect on a relationship is a difficult topic and is something you should discuss with the person you're seeing. The expectations you may have in a relationship involving sex may be quite different from your friend's expectations. You'd better discuss those expectations.

Ideally, if you sleep with someone, you should introduce exclusivity. Why? Because monogamy with someone you know to be disease-free is safer than sleeping with whomever you want at the same time. You are apt to make a mistake, which could lead to infection or possibly a death sentence (vis-a-vis AIDS). Don't just write this warning off as an idle threat; it's good, smart advice. Think *very* carefully about what I'm saying here.

Marriage

Marriage is often the aim for many people who date. Again, this is another one of the expectations to discuss. Some people want to get married, and others just don't. It is not uncommon these days for people to live together indefinitely. They are quite comfortable in such an arrangement and don't see the need to change. Then there are people who have experienced divorce after years of marriage, and have decided they don't want to be married again. If you've never been married, you may want to get married at some time. You hope to meet people, date them, and find your mate, perhaps for life.

But you'll never know how the person you're dating feels about marriage until you bring up the subject. Be direct about it. Then, if she is adamantly averse to marriage, and you know marriage is your main interest, you may decide to stop dating that person. Nonetheless, I do suggest you only bring marriage up when the timing seems right.

No need to bring it up immediately when you first meet someone: "Hi, I'm John, I want to get married, how about you?"

Kids

How do you feel about having children? This is another important topic to discuss with someone you're dating - when the time is right. Once you get to know someone well enough, this is as important as discussing your feelings about marriage.

Do you want children? If you do, do you want your own or are you receptive to raising someone else's (such as the children of the person you marry)? Whatever you do, do not expect that everyone wants to have and raise children. Many people do not. In generations past people just naturally assumed everyone who got married would have two or three kids. This just does not apply any longer. Not all people want the responsibility, the expense, the headaches, whatever.

In the end, always bear in mind that you should search yourself to know what your expectations are. Then you must share those expectations with the person you are getting to know, and find out what her expectations are. If you don't do this, you could be in for an unpleasant surprise someday.

Sex

As I've suggested at various points throughout this book, sex is a complicated matter. For one thing, sex has a way of completely changing the way people relate to each other. Once two people have sex together, everything is different. This can be great and enhance the relationship, or it can complicate things and ruin a relationship. Be careful, and don't expect sex will make things better in the relationship you have with someone.

The moral: when it comes to emotions and feelings, proceed with caution about permitting sex to enter the picture too soon. You may

even decide to end a relationship before sex enters the picture. Women tend to become especially vulnerable when they allow sex to enter the picture too soon. Of course, I realize most often that if sex does not enter the picture sooner or later, the relationship can end for that reason alone. Typically, men will not hang around if sex does not eventually become part of the relationship. Dating and sex have become all the more complicated these days in light of the many venereal diseases transmitted between people. Learn about the diseases, particularly AIDS, which is a death sentence if you get it. Too many people are not careful enough in the dating scene. Here are some guidelines I suggest you consider before you go to bed for the first time with *anyone* you date:

- *Be open with your date, and discuss sex. You want to find out if she has any transmittable diseases. Anyone can be infected, no matter what the education, social orientation, race, etc. Will your partner tell the truth? Maybe, maybe not. But you should try to find out. These days, people are even asking their potential lovers to provide a clean bill of health in the form of a note from a doctor. If you and your date are honest with each other, this may not be necessary. But I actually think it's a smart idea.*

- *Make it clear that your concern is not out of distrust. Rather, you are genuinely concerned about the health and welfare of both of you. Remember: when you go to bed with someone, from a bacterial and viral standpoint, you are going to bed with all her previous partners.*

- *Look for visible signs of infection on your partner (and yourself!). Depending on the disease, if someone is infected, you can identify some telltale signs. For example, look for odd-looking sores, warts, rashes, discharges (pus, blood, or both). It helps to learn about the different types of diseases and symptoms. Briefly, bacterial infections (e.g., gonorrhea, chlamydia, and syphilis) are curable, usually with antibiotics, while viral infections (e.g., genital herpes, genital warts, and AIDS) are incurable. Go to the doctor immediately if you suspect infection. Obviously, you should not have sex with someone who has some type of infection.*

- *Unless you are in a monogamous relationship for several years and know you are infection-free, you should use a condom always. But there is a right way and a wrong way to use a condom. For one thing, the condom should be put on before any sexual activity. Also, don't expose a condom to heat or petroleum-based products - the latex of the condom reacts and can tear or melt. Condoms with spermicide such as nonoxynol-9 can reduce the spread of certain diseases.*

- *Always be aware that someone infected with a sexually transmitted disease is never completely safe to have sex with, no matter what precautions you take.*

What amazes me is the vast numbers of people who take no precautions whatever. According to one survey of college-aged people, as few as 24.8% of the men and 15.6% of the women used a condom during sexual intercourse. This is not smart dating on the part of the rest. In fact, the behavior of the majority is dangerous. Please seriously consider what I have shared with you here about this tricky part of the dating experience in the '90s.

Personal Grooming

Personal grooming may be the most boring topic to you. After all, you know all the things you need to know, right? Maybe you do, maybe you don't. Nonetheless, take heed: what you read here could make the difference between success and failure in the dating scene.

I'll present here what I know are the most important aspects of grooming.

General Appearance for Men and Women

Study the list below to learn about general appearance for men and women. *Check off each query to discover how many things you practice.*

• *Do you bathe every day (especially before a date)?*

• *Do you brush your teeth every day (especially before a date)? Chewing gum instead of brushing does not count. Besides, very often people who are regular gum chewers will pop, snap, and chew like a cow with its cud, much to the annoyance of the date.*

• *Are your ears clean? It may sound strange, but some people don't even know they wander around with wax hanging out of their ears. This is not very appealing.*

• *Do you keep your hair clean, fresh smelling, and well groomed?*

• *Are your clothes clean? You should wear properly fitting clothes, clothes that are fashionable to look good in, and you should keep your clothes smelling fresh. Men are notorious for wearing the same old clothes day in and day out, often neglecting to iron them, which makes clothes look as if they were slept in.*

• *Are your shoes or boots polished? Are your tennis shoes reasonably clean?*

• *Do you dress appropriately for the type of date you're going on?*

---

*Do you bathe every day
(especially before a date)?*

Appearance for Men

Study the list below to learn about proper appearance for men. Again, check off each query so you can discover how many practices you follow.

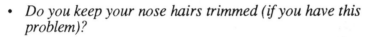

- *Do you keep your beard or mustache trimmed (if this applies, obviously)?*

- *Do you keep clean shaven when you don't normally grow a beard or mustache (again, if this applies to you)?*

- *Do you keep your nose hairs trimmed (if you have this problem)?*

- *Do you keep your ear hairs trimmed or plucked (if this is your problem)?*

- *Do you use a* light *-scented deodorant or cologne?*

- *Do you keep your eyebrow hairs plucked, especially if they tend to grow over your nose?*

- *Do you keep your hands clean and fingernails manicured?*
  Most women are turned off by a man who has grubby hands with dirt or grease under his fingernails. Take the time to take care of this. This also applies to feet and toes, particularly if you like wearing sandals.

Appearance for Women

Study the list below to learn about proper appearance for women. Again, check off each query so you can discover how many of these practices you follow.

- *Do you keep your legs and underarms shaved?*
  If not, you should. Men definitely do not like to see hairy legs and underarms. In other cultures it's no big deal, but in America, it *is* a big deal. Take heed!

- *Do you keep your nose hairs trimmed (if you have this problem)?* Yes, women can have this problem.

- *Do you keep your eyebrow hairs plucked, especially if they tend to grow over your nose?*

- *Do you keep your hands clean and fingernails manicured?*
  Women are generally better about this than men, but I have seen some startling exceptions. Don't be one of them! Again, just as with men, this also applies to feet and toes, particularly if you like wearing sandals.

- *Do you use a lot of makeup?*
  Be careful about this. Most men are not fond of makeup on women. They usually prefer little or no makeup. Some call this "the natural look." Of course, if you know how to apply makeup, you may be skillful enough to accentuate your features with makeup and do so in a way that does not reveal that you are using makeup. This takes skill and practice. There are places to learn how to put on makeup. Some modeling schools teach the use of makeup, or you could ask a professional beautician to teach you.

- *Do you have an attractive hairstyle?*
  Hair is a very important part of a woman's look. Men love hair! Have your hair styled, cut, whatever, in a way that suits your personality. This may be difficult, and it may actually take months to discover just the right style, but hair is well worth the investment to fuss over.

- *Do you keep any unwanted facial hair under control?*
  This is hair you should also make a fuss over. A woman with a mustache or other hair on her face is a definite turn-off for most men. Deal with this if this is your misfortune. You may even look into using electrolysis to deal with the problem. Check the Yellow Pages.

- *Do you wear too much perfume?*
  This is another difficult issue for women, and perhaps as controversial as the overuse of makeup.
  You may *just love* a particular scent, but if it is so strong that it becomes the focal point each time you're in the company of people, you had better tone things down. Another problem is those perfumes which are just *too* sweet-smelling. The trick is to find a scent that is appealing but not overwhelming, and does not linger too long after you leave a room. This can be tricky because perfumes react differently to the body chemistries of different people. Experiment, and have a friend or two help you decide what works.

Other Grooming Concerns

Apart from personal grooming concerns, you should also be concerned about such matters as the general cleanliness and orderliness of your home and automobile.

Believe it or not, your home *is* a reflection of you. It usually doesn't matter too much if your home is old or new, but if your place is a wreck, with stuff all over, and it smells, this could be just enough to turn off a date who has come to visit.

Your car is also a reflection of you. Sometimes the make and model can make a difference (more on this below), but no matter what the year, a clean and fresh automobile can make a big difference about how your dates respond to you.

Now, you may think some of the things on these lists and the attention to cleanliness and orderliness are petty details. Keep in mind, however, that it's the overall impression you are making. Sometimes it is the *little* things that make the difference. And these little things can add up to one big picture. But don't misunderstand, you can have everything proper and in its place, and if you conduct yourself the wrong way, and you say the wrong things, none of these things will probably make any difference.

Physical Fitness

You have probably heard the saying, "Birds of a feather flock together." Well, strange as it may sound, this is true of people in the dating scene. Generally, you'll attract what you look like. If you're overweight and not particularly in tune with your body, you'll probably end up dating people who are overweight and not particularly in tune with their bodies. Conversely, if you are fit, lean, and strong, chances are you'll meet and date people who are fit, lean, and strong.

People who are fit are usually very aware of other people who obviously make the effort to be in good shape. They empathize with each other. Often this can even lead to conversation between them. For example, one runner might notice the fit physique of another person wearing a certain shoe worn by runners and comment on this fact: "Do you run? I'm a runner, and I couldn't help noticing that you are wearing that new Nike running shoe."

Being physically fit is a very good way to prepare yourself for the dating scene. If you are not into physical fitness, and you want to date fit, lean, attractive people, I strongly suggest you start a regimen of physical fitness right away.

Besides, if you have not already heard, exercise is very good for your overall health and frame of mind. You're more alert, more self-assured and confident, and you are actually able to cope with stress more effectively. Also, if you make the effort to exercise regularly, you're not as inclined to be a smoker, a heavy drinker, an overeater, or a drug user. This makes you all the more appealing to be around. It also means you will probably meet more interesting people, and have the better dates.

Tips to Women About Physical Fitness

To men, a woman with a great body and a pleasant personality is often more desirable than a woman whose only real virtue is a pretty face. This should be good news to some women. Why? Because you can do something to improve your body. You can begin a regimen of physical fitness. Yes, it takes discipline, and it may not be that much fun, but you will definitely begin to feel better, and look better, and this will lead to better dates.

Of course, you unfit female readers may think just hiding your body is a good way to deceive men. Big billowy dresses or skirts, giant t-shirts over baggy pants, jogging suits, whatever. This may work some of the time, but in the end, it will not work. Men make an effort to check women out. They want to know if a woman's body looks good. As much as you may not like it, as unfair as you may think it is, and as beastly as you may think men are, this is an inescapable fact. You may hate men because of it, and you may hate women who have great bodies, but this fact still remains. So, get off your duff and work out! (And watch what you eat, too!)

Tips to People in Mid-Life and Beyond

Many people think they are limited to a certain age group they can date. Actually, if you keep yourself in great shape, you can date people many years younger than you. This applies to both men *and* women. I know of some women in their mid-forties and others in their fifties who are in better shape than women nearly twenty years younger than they are. Will they get dates? You bet! In fact, I know as a fact that younger men often find older women very sexy, if those women are in great shape.

Have I convinced you? I couldn't make a better wish for you than that you take responsibility for your physical fitness and make a lifetime commitment to yourself. For suggested reading on fitness, see the Sources section of this book.

Things that Could Make a Difference

Just like your personal appearance and the cleanliness of your home and car, a number of other things can make a difference in your success in the dating scene.

This may seem obvious to some people, and ridiculous to others, but the type of car you drive could make a difference with some people you wish to date. If you drive a sports car, this can be a turn-on for some people, but a turn-off for others. Of course, the same would apply to motorcycles. And then there are people who are Cadillac people, or Corvette people, or even truck people. I guess the rule of thumb is that you can't please everyone. So, the best you can do is drive what you like and can afford, and keep whatever you drive clean.

I touched on keeping your home clean and orderly. Other things to keep in mind include keeping your home comfortable, accommodating guests so they are practically pampered, and keeping away pets that may intrude or bother your guests. These things can make the difference in whether or not your guest would want to come back.

Your level of education could make a
difference with some people you wish to date.

Your level of education could make a difference with some people you wish to date. An education can be formal (college or university, - undergraduate or graduate) or informal (at home reading books). Ultimately, it's not how well educated you are, or even the degree you have attained (although some people are impressed by degrees), as much as it is how interesting you are to talk to. The most attractive type of educated person is someone who has a grasp of many subjects, but does not come across as an arrogant know-it-all.

But what if all you know is sports? If you are a man trying to get acquainted with a woman, you'll probably be a bore if all you can talk about is sports. I suggest you broaden your interests, unless you plan to date only people who are sports-minded like you.

Your bank account can make a difference with someone you wish to date. If you're broke all the time, you may give the impression that you're broke. This is not a very appealing image. But then, if you're rich, you can turn people off by showing off how rich you are. It is always good to have money in your bank account, especially when it's more than you really need. You can feel more self-assured and confident with money in the bank. But don't advertise your wealth. Spend in moderation and never let others know how much you have. Either they will be jealous, or they'll want you to share.

Your occupation can make a difference to the person you wish to date. Some people are drawn to people with fancy titles, or glamorous occupations. It is well known that rock stars have always had women at their beck and call. This is also true of famous sports stars and actors.

Sometimes, it is the prestige of an occupation that makes a person alluring. Some women are attracted to doctors and lawyers because of the respect these people have commanded (although the respect for these professions is declining these days). I know that women were often turned off initially by the fact that I ran a janitorial business. But I would not let them stereotype me as an uneducated person who could do nothing but janitorial work. I take pride in a highly successful company I've run for many years. And after a short discussion with me, anyone can tell that I am not dumb or uneducated.

Keep in mind that whatever you do, you should do it with a passion. Be the best you can be, and you will be rewarded with a sense of pride, a sense of achievement, and adulation from your peers. This will affect your attitude. And a positive attitude will positively affect your dating experience.

Kids and Dating

What do kids have to do with dating? Plenty. These days there are more and more single women and men raising kids. And most of these people are out seeking dates and dating. The problem is that the kids can interfere with their prospects. Why? The fact is, many people of the opposite sex will not even consider dating someone with kids. They just could not be bothered, particularly if the kids are still living at home.

I've had dates admit to me that if my boys were still living with me, they would not date me. They are my sons, and I know they are well behaved, but this seems to be the exception and not the rule. I date women who have kids at home, and I know how trying it can be. The children of some of my dates have done some strange things to me. Unprovoked, their kids have cussed me out, told me to leave their home, spat on me, stolen money from my pocket, lied to me, ignored me, and just been generally obnoxious. What is really strange is that these same kids, who may have spat on me or whatever, can turn around 30 minutes later and behave themselves.

Can I blame people for not dating someone who has kids? No. What should you do when dating someone with kids? As a rule, if you want to continue dating the parent of those kids, no matter how misbehaved the kids may be, say nothing. This can be hard for people with certain temperments. But if you can't say something positive or constructive, just be silent.

People are very strange when it comes to raising their kids. They do whatever they want, and they don't want to hear what anyone else has to say about it.

So the parent you're dating views her kids differently from you. She loves her child, and while you see an obnoxious brat, she sees a child she loves demonstrating a strong, determined spirit. Whatever. If that's how she views it, that's how she views it. There's nothing you can do about it, except perhaps no longer date her.

Of course, bear in mind, if you have kids living at home with you, chances are, if your kids are well behaved, you stand a better chance of sustaining a relationship. This should not be a big surprise. But if your kids fall into the obnoxious category, although you may not think so, don't be surprised if your date does not appreciate your way of parenting.

Also, don't be surprised if you lose dates because of your obnoxious kids. Try to be realistic and accept that your kids are a nuisance to your visiting date. If you keep your kids in line, this could improve your love life dramatically. Discipline is not bad, it's smart. Children actually respect their parents for it in the long run. As for those people who don't date people with kids, they couldn't care less how well behaved your kids are. They just don't want the responsibility of raising someone else's kids, and there's nothing you can do about it.

Dancing:
A Great Way To Meet Dates

I have already given you some excellent direction on where to find dates. In general you learned that you can meet people of the opposite sex everywhere, and chance encounters can lead to dates. But you have also learned that you can meet dates through friends and possibly even through some hobby. As I've said, hobbies can be the easiest and the most enjoyable way to meet dates. And of all the hobbies I know of, dancing is perhaps one of the best hobbies or social activities that can lead to dates. For this reason, I have devoted this whole chapter to dancing as a means to finding dates.

Now, initially, you may object to the idea of going dancing to meet dates. Men are often not especially enthusiastic about dancing. But I wish to encourage you to bear with me here. Please don't underestimate the potential for making new friends and meeting dates while dancing. Besides, I'll walk you through this sometimes strange singles scene, step by step, to keep you comfortable. And for you readers who already dance, perhaps I can provide some pointers to improve your success at meeting dates.

Learning To Dance

Men, do you dance well? If you do, you'll be in great demand by the women because most men don't dance well. But don't worry, if you need help learning to dance, here are several ways to fix that:

1. *Friends or relatives who know how to dance can help you learn.*

2. *You can take professional lessons at dance studios. Check the Yellow Pages under Dancing. Some studios even arrange special outings to dance clubs so you can get a feel of dancing in the real world.*

3. *Free or inexpensive lessons at large dance clubs are available. Check the Yellow Pages under Nightclubs, and call around.*

Now, don't hesitate to use all of the above if that's what it takes for you to have confidence when you dance. Also, the more dances you learn, the more fun you'll have and the more popular you'll be with the opposite sex. Besides, if a woman you want to dance with doesn't know a particular dance, you'll be able to teach her or catch her on another song.

Hey guys (don't read this, women), women are always impressed with the men who know how to dance. They'll think you are so-o-o-o romantic and suave. Really! I know what I'm talking about here. Ask a woman if this isn't so - your mother, sister, neighbor, any woman. That's one of the reasons why dancing is one of my favorite hobbies. Furthermore, I happen to be a music lover, and dancing is a great way to appreciate music.

For my female readers, although you do usually dance better than we men, men are not jealous. No. In fact, we love to watch you move on the dance floor - it's so-o-o-o sensuous. If you don't believe me, ask any man if he likes watching women dance - his smile will convince you just how much!

Where Should You Go To Dance?

Okay, we're going to go dancing, but where do we go? The answer to this will vary from person to person, depending on such things as age and music preference. I happen to like most music: blues, rock, reggae, country, or just oldies. They're all good to me. Also, where you go dancing depends on what is available in your area. Fortunately, I live in an area where there is a dance place to accommodate each kind of music I like. Now, I don't ballroom dance, but my mother used to meet dates of her own while ballroom dancing. In fact, if you like ballroom dancing, there are clubs that cater to ballroom dancing even in the '90s.

Again, I recommend that you learn a variety of dances. This is not as hard as it may sound. For one thing, all dances have a lot in common, which makes it easier to learn dances in the first place, and ultimately enables you to be better at the dances you learn. This will make you more flexible no matter where you are. Moreover, you'll have more confidence, and it will be very impressive to potential dates (those watching you dance) and to dates you happen to take dancing.

I admit, it could take years to learn and become skilled at dancing dozens of dances. But remember: dancing is an investment in your future. Indeed, dancing is a valuable social grace. And once you learn to dance, like swimming or riding a bike, it is something you'll have for the rest of your life to enjoy. Believe me, if you become a good dancer, you will never lack for dates. Women ask me out to dance all the time, just to go dancing. True, it may not necessarily be a romantic date, but it's definitely a fun evening with a friend.

How To Dress For Dancing

The rule of thumb is to dress for the type of dance club you will be visiting. It is not hard to do: just go to observe what others wear at a particular dance club. For example, if you go to a country western dance club, you'll discover that a three-piece suit just doesn't fit. And you would feel out of place wearing blue jeans if you went to a classy night club.

Another thing to bear in mind is that the opposite sex does notice what you wear. If you make an error in what you wear, it's better to go overdressed than inadequately dressed.

My advice for dress is that you spend some time visiting a number of dance clubs and bars. At first go only to get a sense for the ones where you feel most comfortable. Notice what people are wearing for the most part. You will see quickly how much dress differs from club to club. To help, you may even consider starting a notebook to keep a record of what you find. This way you can go back to your notebook if you are in doubt about what to wear to a particular dance club. Believe me, you'll have a lot more fun if you feel you fit in.

Finally, I advise that you commit yourself to pay whatever it takes to get some nice clothing to wear dancing. It pays to look the part and look good.

Drinking & Dancing

You only have about 30 seconds to make a good first impression. No need to ruin that first impression by having only half a brain functioning. People do not like to meet drunks, or even those who are obviously on their way to being drunk. I know from personal experience that the less I drink, the more successful I am in the dancing and dating scene. By the way, this also applies to the avoidance of illegal drugs.

*...if you really want to meet the more desirable dates,
don't drink.*

These days, it is not unacceptable to avoid drinking, even while
visiting a bar or night club where drinks are normally served. And if
you really want to meet the more desirable dates, don't drink. Sure,
drunk or stoned people may be more inclined to accept you, but this is
not what this is all about.

Just remember:

- *Drunks don't dance well*
- *Drunks will not be able to follow the important steps to getting a date*
- *Drunks are usually not a delight to talk to*
- *Most people get a little obnoxious when drunk*
- *You can't drive safely when drunk.*

Before you go out, you will have to decide on the purpose of your evening. Are you out for a good time with the boys or girls, or do you want to meet a potentially exciting date?

Going To Your Chosen Dance Club

When you arrive at the dance club, be really particular about where you sit. It is important to select a seat near the dance floor and yet stay in a position where you can observe the rest of the club. Eventually, you'll learn how early to arrive to have a good pick of the seats.

Let's assume you have a good seat. Now, what you want to achieve here is to *see and be seen*. Watch as others come in. Are they alone, or already with a date? Here is something you should know: sometimes a person will go out dancing with a friend of the opposite sex, but they are not dating - a fact which can only be determined if you pay close attention.

By sitting close to the dance floor, others can see you when they get up to dance. Furthermore, you will be able to see the dancers and discover how good everyone is. As you evaluate the dancers, you'll have to determine if you need to be careful with a particular dancer, or if you want her to teach you some new steps? Another advantage of being close to the dance floor is that it's a great place to flirt - the one time a little direct eye contact or "creative staring" is not out of place.

Here's a sneaky tip: if you are with a friend, let him/her sit with his/her back to the dance floor (or take turns), and you make sure you take full advantage of being seen. In case you doubt the effectiveness of this tip, sit away from the dance floor in a secluded area and notice the difference.

A Few Tips On Being Observant

From your choice observation seat, here are a few more things you should be watching for:

1. Does the man or woman have on a wedding ring?

Be aware that many married people go out dancing without their spouses, because their spouses don't like dancing. I've learned that most of the time it is the wife who's out dancing and not the husband. Men generally don't like dancing.

It's okay to dance with married people. Just be sure you treat them with respect. Then, next time they see you out dancing, they will remember how nice you were with them. This could open up opportunities:

A. They may actually be separated and not ready to admit to it yet, or perhaps they are looking for some side action. (If you discover that it is the latter of these two possibilities, *I strongly urge you to run!*)

B. They may bring a single friend with them and introduce you with a good word.

2. Is the person you're interested in showing obvious signs of enjoying the music by bouncing in time to the music or by keeping time with her feet or fingers?

Nine times out of ten, this is a good indication that she wants to dance.

3. Spot the person you are interested in, and observe what and how that person is drinking.

The fact is that you'll immediately spot who you would like to dance with. But don't jump up and run over to her right away, particularly if she just entered the dance club. Give her a chance to relax and loosen up a bit. Let her finish the first drink and order a second before asking her to dance.

But isn't drinking a problem? If she wants to dance, it will be obvious by how she responds to the music, as I've said above. You probably don't have to be concerned that she is there to get drunk. The point here is to give the person a chance to unwind and get into being at the club. Quite frankly, most men make a pest of themselves at this point. They spot a good-looking woman and spring into action. If you watch closely, these guys will be turned down. At first the turn down makes the woman look as if she is playing hard-to-get. In reality, she just needs time to relax. Then, after enough time has passed, she will appreciate a man's attention a lot more.

How To Ask For A Dance

You could ask for a dance in a lot of different ways. For example, you could be very sophisticated and say something witty and charming like, "Hi, wanna dance?" If that person wants to dance, you'll get a dance out of her, in spite of yourself.

When asking for a dance, I recommend you try a more courteous approach like, "Hi, I saw you dancing earlier, and I'd like to dance this song with you." Or maybe, "You're a great dancer, could I have this one with you?" Believe me, it's hard to turn down a dance with someone who's just offered an invitation to dance in such a way. It is what you say *and* how you say your invitation to dance that makes the difference between you and the rest of the crowd. You're not just spouting words. There's a certain attitude delivered.

You may find it interesting to know that I learned this approach to asking for a dance from women who have used it on me.

Obviously, if you have spotted a person you're interested in, but have not seen her dance, you can't use the prescribed invitations to dance. However, you might try one of these to see which feels more comfortable for you:

"Hi, I really like this song, and if you do, too, I'd like to dance with you."

I know this doesn't sound really clever, but if I actually do like the song, this comes across as very sincere. Remember: it's the attitude delivered that can make the difference. A sincere approach is often an effective approach.

Here's another invitation to dance you can try if the person you're interested in is bouncing in her seat:

"You look like you're enjoying this song already right where you're sitting, but would you like to dance with me on the dance floor?" This one always brings some laughter.

Okay, here's one more invitation for you to try:

"Hi, how are you this evening? I'd like to dance to this song with you, how about it?"

Again, this last invitation sounds simple. But is it? Consider this:

---

1. In the delivery of this invitation you showed some manners by asking how she was doing.

2. You said you would like to dance with her, which is a compliment because you singled her out of the crowd.

3. Your delivery was sincere and not just words blurted out without much thought.

Ultimately, you want to avoid the usual, hackneyed invitation: "You wanna dance?"

Men Take Note!

After you have made your invitation to dance, and the woman you've asked accepts, what happens next?

Whatever you do, don't just turn around and head for the dance floor. You could be greatly surprised and embarrassed if you turn around to discover you're out there all by yourself. Keep in mind that you should allow the woman to lead you to the dance floor. Never turn your back to the woman. It is very impolite. I've seen all too many men make fools of themselves because of their lack of manners in this regard.

Being Turned Down

Accept it as a fact that you are going to be turned down every so often. But if someone does turn you down, even when you are as polite and charming as can be, please don't, don't, don't take it personally! I know this may be hard on your ego, but it is time to be mature and accept "no" as a simple expression of desire at the moment. You never know, but there may be many reasons why the person you've invited to dance says "no." Keep in mind, however, that any of those reasons could change within the next 15 minutes. So be polite, and you'll be surprised at how often she will say "yes" later on.

It is an interesting fact that once you do get a "no" from a person you really want to dance with, rest assured that she will be more aware of you. Perhaps you can now understand the advantage of demonstrating your best calm and mature behavior.

Ask One Person To Dance At A Time

Suppose you spot someone you would like to dance with, but she is sitting at a table crowded with people? By all means, don't try to be all things to all people in such an instance. Just focus on that one person you want to dance with. Of course, it is nice and polite to acknowledge the others present: offer at least a smile and perhaps a nod of the head to everyone. But make it easy for them to understand whom you want to ask for the dance. However nice you may think it may be, it is not very effective or sensible to say:

"Would any of you like to dance?"

The fact is that this does not really compliment anyone sitting there, and chances are pretty good none of them will even respond to the invitation. Also, I personally feel it is less awkward to move on politely if your invitation is rejected by one person. This way you won't feel obliged to ask someone else at the same table.

By the way, I learned this one the hard way several years ago. Some friends and I happened to be seated next to a table that had six equally attractive women. I thought this was very convenient for me, so when a song came on that I liked, I turned to the woman closest to me and asked her to dance. When she turned me down, I asked the next woman, then the next, and the next, until the entire table had turned me down. Whew-w-w-w-w! My friends joked and laughed, declaring that I probably had set a world record for getting turned down so many times in a row. I had to laugh with them.

Getting More "Yesses"

If you frequent a particular dance club, eventually many of the faces will become familiar. You, of course, become familiar to them. The advantage of this is that although they may not know you, the recognition does tend to make people more comfortable with the idea of dancing with you. But if you go to a place where the faces are not so familiar to you, you can still get more acceptances to your invitations to dance. Here are some tips that can help:

1. Simply ask people sitting next to the dance floor.

Usually, if someone is sitting right next to the dance floor, she is really into music and dancing. She is least likely to sit in some corner of the dance club. However, such women are not necessarily the people you want to dance with and get to know for the purpose of developing a dating relationship. Instead, these people can be very effective in helping you receive attention. As you dance, those people whom you really want to get to know will see you dance.

So, dance with the *serious* dancers; have a good time. Then, after a few dances, the people you really want to dance with and get to know will probably have had enough time to relax. They've also had time to see what you have to offer. Once you come along, dancing with you may seem like a good idea.

2. *Watch for people who are probably especially eager to dance and ask them to dance first.*

You can identify these people by their enthusiasm for the music - the bouncing in the seat, the tapping of feet, the snapping or drumming of fingers, singing, etc.

3. *Watch for people who are already doing a lot of dancing - they're there to dance!*

4. **When you go to a table that has several people, and one is really pretty, pick one of the others to dance with first.**

The pretty one will probably be pleasantly surprised, and therefore more eager to dance with you when you come around to ask her.

Now, you might say to this: "Come on, does that really work?" You bet it does! In fact, this one really works well for both men *and* women. You'll even discover that you get turned down much less frequently, which is good for your ego and confidence. More importantly, however, you'll discover:

A. You spend more time on the dance floor having fun. Which has an almost magical way of attracting others to you who also want to dance.

B. For men, the more you dance with different women, the more you send out a signal to all women that you're there to dance, and not just to score. And since you came to dance and have fun, this makes you a lot "safer" in the eyes of nearly all women.

Once in a while the person you ask to dance will turn you down, but then suggest you dance with her friend. While this is not good manners on her part, play the hero and graciously follow the lead. The worst that can happen is that you dance with someone you really don't care for. Still, in the process, you continue to show how adaptable and in control you really are.

Bear in mind that all these suggestions are intended for your benefit. They should make your experience in the dancing scene more comfortable, enjoyable, and successful. Therefore, don't stray too far off from these suggestions.

My Ugly Story

You should be aware that nearly everyone has an unfortunate experience sooner or later in the dancing scene. I don't want you to be discouraged or frightened off by this, I just want you to be aware that it can happen. Let me relate to you one of my ugly stories.

One of my good buddies and I were sitting in one of the more popular oldies dance clubs in our area, when he spotted this cute woman he wanted to dance with. My buddy waited long enough for one of his favorite songs to play and then quickly went to her to ask for a dance. To the surprise of both of us, she shook her head and pointed to me. My buddy returned to our table, not at all mad, and said, "She wants to dance with you." We both had to laugh at this women's rudeness. Still, I got up and danced with her.

The dance went well, and I sat down gratified, but still a little puzzled over how this woman treated my friend. Eventually, a little later, this same woman got my attention, wiggling her finger for me to dance with her again. Naturally, I obliged. I continued to dance with her three times in a row, then returned to my table.

I let some time pass, and this time when I heard a song I liked, I thought it natural to ask this woman for a dance. I very politely asked her for the dance, and much to my surprise she rather rudely said flat "No." Evidently she wanted to talk to her female friend. Fine, I thought, I'll try later.

About 30 minutes passed, and I tried again with this same woman. The conversation went something like this:

"Are you ready to dance, yet?" I asked, smiling and saying this in as agreeable a way that I knew how.

"No, I'm not," she fired back.

Then, quite unexpectedly, her friend got out of her seat and, standing squarely before me, exclaimed:

"What part of 'no' don't you understand?!"

Needless to say, I was astounded at this obnoxious display. I was not angry, nor was I intimidated, and I very calmly replied:

"I think I understand *this* 'no'!"

The lesson my friend and I learned here was that when a person is rude to one person, sooner or later she'll probably treat everyone rudely. That's just the way it is. The lesson to you, my reader, is that you will encounter some things that you must simply take in stride and accept as part of learning life's lessons.

Dancing And Asking For A Date

I hope my readers, who are not particularly thrilled about dancing, are still with me. At the very least you're probably wondering when I will get to the part about asking people out for a date at a dance club. Keep reading, and I'll reveal what to do and what not to do with regard to the dating game.

Save Your Money

It is fun to buy drinks for others when you're out dancing and partying. I personally like buying for and receiving drinks from women I know. (Yes, it is very common for women to buy drinks for men - when they're with friends.)

However, I learned a long time ago what a waste of money it is just to send drinks over to strangers. I find that many women are very wary of strange men who send over drinks to their tables. I've heard women make several comments on this custom:

"Sure, I'll let a man spend his money - but I'm not inviting him over to my table."

"If he's got money to waste, let him waste it on me, I don't care. But that doesn't mean I'm interested in him."

"Just because he's buying me drinks, doesn't mean I'm going home with him."

Most women are much more impressed by the show of good manners when you ask them for a dance, than the show of money. In a way, such a practice gives the impression that a man is hard up, and it does not help him one bit in getting to know a woman.

Now, after I've become acquainted with a woman, and I've been invited (I haven't invited myself) to sit with her, then I always like to buy drinks for her.

No Talking On The Dance Floor

If you think that to get to know someone at a dance club you should talk to her while you dance with her, you're wrong. You can listen to the music and dance, or even sing along if you want to, but don't try to converse. For one thing, you are not expected to talk, and chances are the music is so loud, you couldn't talk anyway.

Remember this: you asked the person to dance, not talk! Some people (like me) strongly dislike any effort on the part of a dancing partner to talk while dancing. One time I even heard one woman ask some poor guy out loud - very much out loud - if he had come to dance or talk. Not a very enjoyable or enviable situation. So again, just enjoy the music and concentrate on the dance.

Creative Flirting

Flirting is like an expensive perfume - a little can go a long way! And a little is usually very much appreciated. So go ahead, flirt a little. But be genuine and show some feeling. Also, make sure you save most of your flirting for the man/woman you really want to spend more time with.

How do you flirt? Okay, generally, flirting involves things you say and things you do to compliment the other person to let her know you're interested.

As for things you do, usually this takes the form of staring (without your eyes popping out of your head), or just exchanging a look now and then with a person you find attractive. Smiling at someone is also a form of flirting. Here are a few things you could say.

After you've danced with her, you could say:

"I enjoyed dancing with you. Thank you."

Or, you could compliment your dance partner on what she's wearing:

"That's a real nice outfit you're wearing. I like it on you!"

If you are especially attracted to the person, you could compliment her on some physical or character attribute. Such compliments are of the more powerful and effective flirting variety. For example:

"I love your sparkling brown eyes; they're very sexy."

Or this:

"Your sweet personality is very attractive to me."

Bear in mind, these types of compliments should be used sparingly, and only for people whom you want to remember you, because they will.

Also, these flirtatious remarks are really compliments, and we all love them. You should always try to find something positive about someone to say to her as a compliment. If you compliment someone with sincerity, you'll make a lasting impression. Besides, if you really want to get to know someone, this is one way she will know you are definitely interested in her. This will make her feel special, even if you just met. Believe me, this can make it a lot easier to get to know a person.

Finally, whatever type of flirting you employ, don't overdo it. Remember: always keep the other person *comfortable*. And by all means, be sincere.

Careful on Those Slow Dances

Remember the key word: *comfort*. You men must be especially careful. Although I will let you know that some women tend to get too aggressive during slow dances. Anyway, just aim to keep your dance partner comfortable at all times, or she might shy away. This is particularly important when dancing with strangers. They don't know you, so don't push it. Don't dance too close, or attempt to be too "friendly." Men, keep in mind that most women just don't appreciate when a man takes such liberties.

Sure, it feels good to dance close to people, but you have to earn the right to do that. If you push too fast, you'll offend her, and she won't want to get to know you better.

> *...the closeness you want can often happen much
> faster when taking this approach.*

The best way to handle slow dancing is for a man to let the woman lead. You men should take it easy, and demonstrate you are in no hurry to get close. The odd thing is that the closeness you want can often happen much faster when taking this approach. Usually, when a woman feels comfortable with a man, she will put her head close to his face or shoulder.

Here's another important thing to remember: other people are watching. You certainly don't want to scare off other potential dates. Show courtesy, restraint, and finesse. I guarantee, you'll get a lot more slow dances.

Romeos, Stay Home!

Several women friends of mine have told me the same ugly story, although with some variations on the details. Anyway, the scene generally goes something like this:

A man will ask for a slow dance (he could be either a complete stranger or a nominal acquaintance) and will appear quite sincere enough to a woman that she would give him a chance. But the man, being drunk or just a complete ass, will utterly ruin any chances of getting to know this woman, or any others in the dance club, probably forever. This hot-to-trot Romeo will start to lick the earlobe or shoulder of the woman, talk dirty, or possibly press his manhood against the woman. And as if that were not enough, many of these guys follow the woman back to her table and sit down without invitation.

This type of obnoxious and unbelievably stupid behavior is talked about and shared among women at a dance club faster than wild fire. Any man pulling such a stunt is history for any of the women there. He may as well go home and forget it.

Getting A Name

You men, after you have had a good dance and escorted the woman back to her table, you've demonstrated that you can be courteous and fun. If she hasn't already done so, you can now exchange names with the woman and get a little acquainted.

You may wonder: why is this the best way to go about getting acquainted with someone? Here's why:

1. You won't come off seeming overly eager.

It seems some people just have to broadcast their eagerness. But this just turns people off.

2. Now you can concentrate on remembering the name of your new acquaintance.

It's a fact that a woman is impressed when you ask her to dance again. But when you ask her by name, it's even more impressive. Of course, there is a good chance she won't remember your name. That's okay. She might be dancing with more people than you are. Besides, you went back to your table to write her name down (be sure you got this hint!). This will make you seem like a genius. Try this, and you'll hear remarks like, "Wow, you even remembered my name!" And even if she doesn't make that comment, she'll be impressed.

Men: Be A Gentleman With Words

Women really do appreciate a man who shows restraint, control, and refinement. Plain talk? Watch your language. I was known as the original "Foul Mouth Freddy." I still like to use colorful language, but not in mixed company. Why? I found out how much women are turned off by foul language.

You can adopt a simple rule of thumb: uneducated men use an abundance of foul words because they don't know any others.

And men, don't even be tempted to use foul words, even if a woman uses them openly. You never know if a woman is just testing you. Believe it or not, there are some women who just want to see how refined you are. They may cuss with you, but they won't date you. The fact is, women usually do not appreciate strangers who use unrefined language in their company. Why? Remember our operative word: comfort. A woman needs to feel comfortable with a man. This means she needs to know a man can control his use of words.

Added to foul language are dirty jokes and suggestive comments. These are also quite offensive to women. Now, a woman may not say anything right away, but chances are she cringes at it privately. These things make a woman feel uncomfortable.

~ FOUL-MOUTHED WOMEN ~

For my female readers who think cussing with the guys is impressive to them, think again. Men may use every word in the book, but they don't really like hearing foul language or foul anything else coming from a woman. Double standards you say? You bet. I didn't make this up, I'm just telling you the way it is. I remember when a guy said to me one time: "Man! I hate it when a woman says the "F" word more than me. That lady's mouth was foul!"

No, I'm not getting moralistic, nor am I lecturing you. All this is just good advice to help you get an edge in the dating game.

Invitations To Sit At A Table

For those of my readers who really want to have a chance to sit down and talk to the person they're interested in, I've got a method that does work, but not all the time.

The time to attempt to sit with the person you're interested in is when you return to her table from dancing. For men, allow the woman to get back to her table, and then kneel down on one knee next to the table to talk "just a little." What should you say? The topic of your conversation should be just a few words to get acquainted. Nothing involved - you don't know how she will respond to this type of attention. I would not necessarily advise a woman to try this; I'm not sure how lady-like it looks when a woman kneels next to a man's table.

By the way, whatever gender you happen to be, what you should never do is just find a seat and plop your rear down uninvited. Also, never go to your table to grab your drink and then return to someone else's table to set it - or yourself - down if you haven't been invited to do so.

Let me tell you, I know how much it cramps my style when a woman, whom I did not invite to sit at my table, comes and sits. She eventually gets the idea when I excuse myself to go dance with someone else. Let me put it another way: would you like it if a stranger unexpectedly showed up at your home and expected you to entertain him? Exactly. Neither would I. In effect, that's how imposing it can be when someone just decides to invite himself to someone else's table.

You must also understand that if you allow someone to sit at your table, invited or uninvited, others will not come around to visit. They'll probably be courteous and let you enjoy your company. I know I would! So, if you don't want others to stop asking you to dance, don't let someone sit at your table, giving the impression that you've paired up.

Inviting Someone to Sit with You - versus - The Simple Date

Most of the time, when I'm out dancing, I don't ask women to join me. I find it best to ask a woman I'm interested in for a simple date as described in Chapter 2. If a particular woman and I have hit it off, it's not uncommon for her to ask me for a simple date. I find that more and more women are doing this. But this doesn't mean you guys can just sit back and wait until that happens. It may never happen for you.

As I've indicated a moment ago, anytime you invite someone to sit at your table, you have made a tacit statement to all those at the dance club: do not disturb, we've paired up! And you can be sure that the invitations to dance will end. It may seem strange, but the fact is that by inviting someone over to your table, you're forcing her to make a decision about you. She has to decide if she wants to "pair up" with you at the dance club. This is a significant decision, and the person you've invited may not be ready for that. This could make this person uncomfortable. This can also create an awkward situation. Not a good idea.

There are exceptions to what I've just described. For one thing, you may go to a certain club quite often and see the same people there frequently. If you make the effort of becoming the friend of someone, sometimes she will feel comfortable sitting at your table. Unless, however, you want to develop a special relationship with her, make sure you dance with others at the club and encourage her to do the same.

Also, often people will come with one or more friends. This could present a special problem. If you hit it off with someone who is with another friend, and her friend doesn't really like you very much, or perhaps is not especially fond of the people you are with, forget about sitting with them. But this may not be so bad anyway, since most dance clubs are too noisy to talk much. It's much better just to arrange a simple date with the person you want to spend more time with. This way you can avoid competing with the friends she's with, or you're with, or with the noise in the dance club.

~ WOMEN ASKING MEN for a SIMPLE DATE ~

I want to encourage my female readers here. If you have a lot of charisma, personality, and just plain charm, then be sure to adopt the simple date approach. The simple date approach gives you a chance to ply your charms to men who haven't become acquainted with you. All they know about you is how you look and how well (or not so well) you dance. Give the men a chance, and ask them to join you for a cup of coffee at a local restaurant on the way home. You know the technique.

If you're the shy type, or just old-fashioned thinking, I'm telling you, it just doesn't get any simpler than this. I hate to say this, but it's the truth: unless you look like a model (and some women have been blessed in this way), so often the man you're interested in might not ask you out. And there could be plenty of reasons for this even if you *are* a model:

1. *He is too shy to ask you out.*

2. *He doesn't know how to ask you out.*

3. *He's been turned down recently just one too many times (most likely twice in a row) to have the courage to ask you out. He just can't take the chance and get a third rejection.*

You may be pleasantly surprised to discover that a man you are interested in may have already taken special notice of you. But you won't know unless you ask him for a simple date. I know this is true, because it has happened to me.

Men Asking Cocktail Waitresses for a Date

I'll try to keep this as simple as I know how: as a general rule, men should not try to pick up, hit on, or ask out a cocktail waitress. You can tip a cocktail waitress, but don't try anything else. Stop and think about it for a moment..... Cocktail waitresses get the benefits of the very worst of the place night after night. You don't have a good chance at all.

However, if you insist, there is a way to date a cocktail waitress. But it takes time, and there are no guarantees. To begin with, you have to be different and demonstrate this to the waitress. If you go to the same place time after time, tip her well, speak nicely, but don't try anything else with her, then, over time, *she will take special notice of you.* You can count on this.

Also, be aware that your waitress will be keeping an eye on you to see how you treat other women. When the time comes, and she feels *comfortable* around you, she will take the initiative and let you know she's interested. How much time? That depends on you and on her.

When she's ready she will actually come to sit or stand at your table and talk. She may begin by asking you questions about your job or something. This shows she wants to know more about you personally. If the mood, and the time, seems right, you can approach her with the simple date invitation.

If, however, your waitress never comes over to talk to you to learn more about you personally, leave her alone. You will both be happier with this arrangement if you do.

◆◆

Afterword

At this point you should feel more comfortable about what to do to improve your social skills and to have a higher quality social life. By following the guidelines provided in this book, you can be *smart* in your dating experience. Which means you can get better acquainted with people of the opposite sex, feeling confident in what you're doing. You don't need to worry about whether or not you are doing or saying the wrong thing. You will know what to do to make yourself more presentable and desirable to the other gender. In short, you will be more successful. And success has a way of boosting confidence and yielding more success.

What makes the approach outlined here so smart is that it does so without requiring that you be a different person. In fact, you are encouraged to stay comfortable by being yourself as you go about the business of improving your social life. Moreover, you will come to recognize the sense in allowing people you come to know to let them be comfortable just being themselves. Remember: staying comfortable and keeping the people you come to know comfortable at all times is one key to successful dating, romance, and sex.

For those who wish to learn more about some of the topics covered in this book, I have provided an annotated list of books I recommend in the Sources section at the end of this book.

And for those who are curious about why I have managed to date so many people without apparently finding that special someone. The answer to that is that I *do* have a special someone in my life, and I hope someday to have a successful second marriage. But my experience has been quite varied. I have dated women who only wanted to be friends with no further commitment, others with whom all the details were not worked out, or the kids chased me off, or I wasn't ready for a lasting relationship, etc. It was never my aim to date as many women as I have. Life has a way of taking many odd twists and turns, and you never really know what to expect around the next bend. But then, that's what makes life interesting and worth living.

I hope you benefit from my experience and have a rewarding and fun experience as you pursue a better social life. Best wishes and good luck!

Sources

If you wish to learn more about some of the topics discussed in this book, please consult the material I recommend in this section.

Beyond Codependent, Melody Beattie
Melody Beattie's books are easy reading and address a very difficult part of life - how to experience normal, functional, and healthy relationships. The other Beattie book I recommend is listed below.

Codependent No More, Melody Beattie

Fit or Fat, Covert Bailey
A must read for those who want to make a serious lifetime commitment to staying physically fit. If you think you understand what exercise is all about, but have not read this book, you probably still have a few things to learn This is a very technical book, but is written so simply and full of humor, everyone can enjoy it.

Habitudes, Leland Val VanDeWall (Xoces Publications, Inc., Alberta, Canada, T5K1V9, Telephone: 403/482-4412)
This is a set of audio tapes which can change your life for the better. These tapes contain powerful material which can compel you to become a more positive person, capable of enhanced insight about other people.

How to Make Love All the Time, Barbara DeAngeles
A great book that is full of love you can feel.

Increased Human Effectiveness, Bob Moawad (Edge Learning Institute, Telephone: 1-800/858-1484)

This set of audio tapes are my favorite. These tapes are humorous, sensitive, and contain great insight about human nature. These tapes will teach you to appreciate yourself and others with a new awareness you may not have thought possible.

Love, Leo F. Buscaglia, Ph.D

Leo Buscaglia's books are so clearly and simply written you can't possibly miss his point. Buscaglia's books can help you learn to have a fuller appreciation of yourself as a unique person and how to experience a richer relationship with others. The other books I recommend by Leo Buscaglia are listed below alphabetically.

Love Secrets for a Lasting Relationship, Harold H. Bloomfield, M.D.

This cleverly designed book identifies relationship problems on each open page, and what to do about each problem addressed, including some very wise suggestions. Simple problems (e.g., how you and your partner can make simple decisions together) and complex problems (e.g., how to overcome feelings of rejection) of all types are explored.

Loving Each Other, Leo F. Buscaglia, Ph.D

Personhood, Leo F. Buscaglia, Ph.D

Singled Out, Richard Schickel

A short, humorous book written about the new sexual life and emotions of men after divorce.

The Art of Intimacy, Thomas P. Malone, M.D. & Patrick T. Malone, M.D.

This book will not only give you a clear understanding of what true intimacy is, but can also help you learn to experience intimacy. This is a very technical book, and is not easy to read. However, this book is so good, it is worth reading ten times if that's what it takes to understand this profound book.

The 7 Habits of Highly Effective People, Steven R. Covey

A how-to book that can actually help you become more effective in relationships, work, or anything.

The Hearts That We Broke Long Ago, Merle Shain

This book is endorsed by Leo F. Buscaglia - that says it all!

The Way of the Bull, Leo F. Buscaglia, Ph.D

Women's Encyclopedia of Health & Emotional Healing, Denise Foley et al. (1993, Rodale Press, Emmaus, Pennsylvania)

This is an excellent book intended for women, but it's so informative and interesting, I urge men to read it. This is the source from which I got my information and statistics about sexually transmitted diseases (see pages 439 - 445).

Index

About the Author

In a way, Donald Black was just like anyone else who had ever entered the dating scene - he had no clue about how to meet and get dates. But Donald Black had an uncanny sense of how to get acquainted with people. So, when he began dating again after a failed 16 year marriage, he started to write down his experiences. From this base Black developed a foolproof method for dating that has resulted in this book, *Smart Dating*.

Black *is* a dating guru after a decade of dating dozens of women. He has learned a lot about how men and women relate to each other and knows what works and what doesn't. Black makes his home in Auburn, California where he continues to write on the subjects of dating and romance.

Smart Dating Seminars®

Would you like to meet the author and learn directly from him secrets and techniques to successful dating, romance, and sex? You can by attending one of his *Smart Dating Seminars*®.

Donald Black's Smart Dating Seminars cover:

- *An overview of dating (how to find dates, how to ask someone to a simple date/first date, topics of conversation, grooming, etc.)*

- *Open general audience questions and answers.*

- *Personal one-on-one attention with Donald Black to answer your specific questions.*

Donald Black is also available for speaking engagements. For further information about having Donald Black give a talk, or for information about attending one of his *Smart Dating Seminars*®, call toll free: **1-800-798-2025.**

Order Form

To order additional copies of *Smart Dating: A Guide For Men & Women to Dating, Romance, & Sex,* or to subscribe to the *Smart Dating Newsletter* fill out form and mail to:

PAPER CHASE PRESS
5721 MAGAZINE ST, SUITE 152
NEW ORLEANS LA 70115

Please send me _____ copy(ies) of *Smart Dating: A Guide For Men & Women to Dating, Romance, & Sex* @ $14.95 each.

I wish to subscribe for _____ year(s) to the *Smart Dating Newsletter* @ $12.50 per annual subscription (regularly $25.00 per year). Postage is included with this price.

NAME:_____

ADDRESS:_____

_____

Send check or money order in U.S. funds, payable to PAPER CHASE PRESS.

For shipping & handling, add $1.80 for each book ordered in the U.S.
($4.00 for S&H outside U.S.). For orders in Louisiana, add 9% sales tax.
Allow 4 to 6 weeks for delivery.

Call or write to request a discount sheet for purchases exceeding 10 books.

800-798-2025